Genealogical Research and Resources

A GUIDE FOR LIBRARY USE

by Lois C. Gilmer

American Library Association
CHICAGO AND LONDON
1988

Lois C. Gilmer is director of the library at the University of West Florida at Fort Walton Beach. She has been interested in genealogical research from the perspective of both librarian and researcher for many years.

Designed by Charles Bozett

Composed in Baskerville by
Imperial Printing

Printed on 50-pound Glatfelter,
a pH-neutral stock, and bound
in Strathmore Americana 80-
pound cover stock, by Imperial
Printing

Gilmer, Lois C.
Genealogical research and resources : a concise guide for library use / by Lois C. Gilmer.
p. cm.
Includes bibliographies and index.
ISBN 0-8389-0482-3
1. Libraries--Special collection--Genealogy. 2. Genealogy--Bibliography--Methodology. 3. Genealogy--Bibliography.
4. Reference books--Genealogy--Bibliography. I. Title.
Z688.G3G54   1988   026'.9293–dc19   87-32534

For Mac

Remember the days of old,
Consider the years of many generations:
Ask thy father, and he will shew thee;
Thy elders, and they will tell thee.

                              —Deuteronomy 32:7

Contents

Acknowledgments

The author is indebted to Ms. Connie Works, senior word processing systems operator in the Office of the Vice President for Academic Affairs at the University of West Florida, for typing the manuscript for this book and to Dr. Douglas Friedrich, vice president, and his predecessor, Dr. Arthur Doerr, for making this service available to employees of the university. The author also greatly appreciates the assistance of her editor, Ms. Bettina MacAyeal, and the indulgences of her co-workers and family.

Introduction

At some time almost all of us have had at least a mild curiosity about our ancestors. What nationality were they? Did they come over on the *Mayflower*, or did they, as Will Rogers once said of his family, "Meet the boat." Genealogy is, in fact, one of the most popular hobbies in the United States today. It is also now being studied seriously by students of history.

Many amateurs wanting to conduct their own research turn to librarians for help. Librarians who work in libraries that lack extensive historical and genealogical materials admit that they are at a loss on how to guide people in their search for information about their ancestors. To help fill this need, this book provides basic information on research methodology and organization, as well as on sources that are helpful in conducting a logically ordered search.

Designed as a concise guide, this book does not provide definitive answers to questions, but instead serves to direct searchers to sources of possible answers. An effort has been made to arrange classes of genealogical materials in the order in which research should actually be conducted. While the list of recommended sources cannot be exhaustive, it is representative of the types of materials available. Many of the titles mentioned will be familiar to librarians who have used them in other contexts. The level of treatment is appropriate for the amateur researcher as well; therefore, busy reference librarians may confidently suggest the approach used here to all interested patrons. It is hoped that this short work will help the librarian (1) to pose better questions during reference interviews, (2) to advise patrons of the sources available in their library and of how to best use them, and (3) to refer patrons to other libraries, archives, and organizations.

Chapter 1

Genealogical Reference Service

USING THE LOCAL LIBRARY

Any library can offer important service to the amateur genealogist by connecting him or her to the larger world of collected genealogical materials. However, most local libraries hold materials that can be used for genealogical research, whether or not they were purchased for that purpose. The basic catalogs, reference materials, and encyclopedias owned by even the smallest libraries are helpful and can be used with the essential bibliographies and other historical materials owned by larger libraries.

Therefore, the librarian should not begin by referring the patron to a larger library or to a special genealogical library without first exploring with the patron research possibilities in the library to which he has come for help. Because genealogy and history are inseparable, the genealogist should be treated as an historian. Sources helpful to the historian will be helpful to the genealogist as well.

Library Orientation

Before moving on to the reference interview between the librarian and the amateur genealogist, it should be emphasized that basic library skills are essential to successful genealogical research. Because of the time-consuming nature of genealogical work, many amateur genealogists are retired persons. Often this means that they were never taught basic library skills, or they have forgotten them. Therefore, it is possible that the greatest service a librarian can give to some of these patrons is instruction in library use. The librarian may need to introduce patrons to the public catalog and to other indexes in library collections, as well as to the classification systems peculiar to the library.

1

It would be helpful to the patron and to the librarian if materials specifically prepared for the education of the library user could be given to the patron. Especially helpful for the genealogy patron are pathfinders, or guides, that outline a search strategy and introduce step by step the subject headings, call numbers, and resources available on the subject in the library and beyond. (See figure 1.)

It would also be helpful if an abbreviated classification schedule, such as the *LC Classification: Outline*, could be given to the patron with appropriate categories highlighted.

Even after receiving these preliminary instructions and materials, the patron should be assisted in using the public catalog. From *Sears' List of Subject Headings* or the *Library of Congress Subject Headings*, or any other subject heading list peculiar to the specific library, appropriate terms should be chosen with the patron before beginning the search in the public catalog. In addition to general subjects, such as GENEALOGY, U.S.—GENEALOGY, [Any State]—GENEALOGY, or [Any Country]—GENEALOGY, family names should be looked up. In this way the catalog is being used as a bibliography of books written on the subject and held within that library.

The Reference Interview

The first question to ask a novice researcher is, "What is the name of the family being researched?" While this question may sound elementary, it, nevertheless, forces the patron to "narrow the topic" and concentrate on one family name at a time rather than browse for any name with which he or she may have connections. The second question to be answered is, "Has a family genealogy already been written?" It is possible that a family history only a generation or two removed from the patron has already been written, and he or she is not aware of its existence. It is also possible, because of intermarriage, etc., that the patron's family line is partially covered in a genealogy of another family by a different name. Before any research project is attempted, a literature search should be conducted to determine if work has already been done.

In libraries with genealogical collections, a good place to begin is among the genealogies already on the shelves. By browsing, a patron may discover family histories not found in a search of the public catalog. Genealogies going back several generations include many family names not indexed as subject headings in the public catalog. If the foregoing process fails to reveal a written genealogy, bibliographies may direct the user to an answer.

An introduction to genealogy appears in *Encyclopaedia Britannica*, 11th ed.

Books dealing with this topic are listed in the card catalog under these subjects:
Genealogy
U.S.—Genealogy
(Any state)—Genealogy
(Any country)—Genealogy
Specific family names

General classification numbers covering this subject are:
DDC 929.1
CS (Library of Congress)
GS 4.2 (Superintendent of Documents)

Journal articles of a general nature can be located in periodical indexes under the subject:
Genealogy

Journal articles of a more specialized nature can be located in the following periodicals (under family name):
American Genealogist
Genealogical Helper
Genealogical Journal
Genealogist
New England Historical and Genealogical Register
Virginia Genealogist

Bibliographies that list books and articles on the topic include:
*American and English Genealogies in the Library of Congress, Cata-
logue of Genealogical and Historical Works: Library of the National
Society of the Daughters of the American Revolution*
Index to Printed Pedigrees
Genealogical Books in Print
Biography and Genealogy Master Index

Other specialized collections that include information on this topic are:
Genealogy Libraries
Government Documents
Local History (housed separately or in a special collections department)
Manuscripts (housed separately or in a special collections department)
Rare Books (housed separately or in a special collections department)
Special Collections Department

Figure 1. Steps to Finding Materials on Genealogy

Bibliographies

There are a number of noteworthy bibliographies available specifically for genealogical sources and arranged by thousands of family names. Some of the bibliographies are quite old, with the sources listed therein being even older. Charles Bridger's *Index to Printed Pedigrees*, for example, which was reprinted in 1969, was originally published in 1876. *American and English Genealogies in the Library of Congress* was published in 1919. Several editions of Durrie's *Bibliographia Genealogica Americana: An Alphabetical Index to American Genealogies and Pedigrees Contained in State, County, and Town Histories, Printed Genealogies, and Kindred Works* were published from 1868 to 1908. *The Grafton Index of Books and Magazine Articles on History, Genealogy, and Biography Printed in the United States on American Subjects During the Year 1909* was published in 1910. *Munsell's Genealogical Index* was published in 1933. The *Catalogue of Genealogical and Historical Works: Library of the National Society of the Daughters of the American Revolution* was published in 1940.

Later works are represented by the *National Union Catalog of Manuscript Collections*, which began publication in 1959. A supplement to *Genealogies in the Library of Congress* was published in 1977, and *A Complement to Genealogies in the Library of Congress* was published in 1981. The *Biography and Genealogy Master Index* is another publication of the 1980s.

Most of the titles listed in the genealogy bibliographies will probably be out of print, and patrons must locate them in libraries that already own copies. Netti Schreiner-Yantis has written several editions of *Genealogical Books in Print* for the patron or the librarian who would like to purchase copies of genealogical books.

For current bibliographies on genealogy, including titles of published family histories, R. R. Bowker publications such as *Subject Guide to Books in Print* and *Forthcoming Books* can be used.

Some genealogy books that were out of print are being reprinted because of popular demand. The *Guide to Reprints: An International Bibliography of Scholarly Reprints* is an annual listing of a variety of materials available in reprint form from various publishers. The list of publishers includes Gale Research Company and the Genealogical Publishing Company, both active in publishing genealogical materials.

Genealogical journals also publish, often in installments, genealogies of American families. Some of the best are *The American Genealogist*, *The Genealogical Helper*, *The Genealogical Journal*, *The Genealogist*, *The New England Historical and Genealogical Register*, and *The Virginia Genealogist*. These all are devoted to family genealogies as well as to genealogical services, forms, "how to" articles, queries, and advertisements from professional genealogists. Volume 3 of the Gale Genealogical and Local History Series titled *A Survey of American Genealogical Periodicals and Periodical Indexes*, published in 1978, helps to identify retrospective materials located in genealogical periodicals. See Chapter 4 for more information on periodicals and periodical indexes.

If a published genealogy is found, it should be checked for authenticity. Often a genealogy is pieced together from memories of any number of different people without proper documentation. If the genealogy has been done correctly, the documentation accompanying it can be checked to determine if it is, indeed, based on fact. If the facts are correct, and the researcher can easily tie in his or her family line, his or her work may be feasibly undertaken.

LOCATING MATERIALS IN OTHER COLLECTIONS

Special Libraries

The world's largest genealogy library is the Library of the Genealogical Society of the Church of Jesus Christ of Latter-day Saints. Located in Salt Lake City, Utah, it has a network of branches throughout the world. Searchers who are not members of the church are invited to use the vast resources of this group.

Washington, D.C., is still the nation's genealogical research center, however, with several large libraries located there. The National Archives and Records Service is the main repository of federal records from all three branches of the government. Among the records contained in the National Archives, the federal census, military service and related records, records of federal land transactions, and immigrant arrival records are the most useful to genealogists. The Library of the Daughters of the American Revolution specializes in materials of colonial America and records compiled by local DAR chapters throughout the country.

The Local History and Genealogy Room of the Library of Congress has an extensive collection of genealogies and other sources useful in compiling genealogies, such as immigration records, records of wars, etc. Other collections in the library, such as rare books and manuscripts, newspapers, directories, and maps, also are useful for genealogical research. Free bibliographies are distributed by the Library of Congress.

Membership in the National Genealogical Society entitles one to borrow materials from their library by mail. Since it is often very difficult to obtain genealogical materials on loan, a serious researcher would be well advised to join the society.

Special Collections in Local Libraries

A library in the locale being researched would probably be the best one to consult first. Local collections such as cemetery and church records, old family records, land and town records, and even genealogies that have been compiled by local people can provide the preliminary information needed before checking in offices at county courthouses. These holdings may not be represented in databases or union lists, but interlibrary loan policies at the local level may be more liberal.

Government Depository Collections

For the past two hundred years, the United States government has maintained and published records about the people who have inhabited this country. The list of depository libraries appears annually in the September issue of the *Monthly Catalog of Government Publications*. Guides to the holdings of the National Archives and of the Library of Congress, and copies of census records or information on how to obtain copies may be found in these library collections. The GS 4.2 section in a government documents collection may be browsed for genealogical information.

Out-of-Print Book Dealers

Out-of-print books on family history that cannot be located in a library are often very difficult to find any other place or to obtain when found. They may, however, be located in bookstores that specialize in rare books. Out-of-print dealers will search for the books, charging for their services. Very helpful in locating out-of-print genealogy books are Jonathan Sheppard Books, Albany, New York; Genealogists Bookshelf, New York, New York; and Tuttle Antiquarian Books, Rutland, Vermont. Names of additional out-of-print dealers may be obtained from *AB Bookman's Weekly* and *Antiquarian Book Monthly Review*.

If the out-of-print book can neither be obtained from a library nor bought from a dealer, there is yet another avenue to be pursued. University Microfilms in Ann Arbor, Michigan, can supply microfilm or photocopies of out-of-print family histories. Though this is an expensive solution, the genealogy patron may welcome it.

LOCATING A GENEALOGIST

If the patron does not locate a published genealogy, or if the one found is filled with obvious errors, the patron will need to start compiling her or his own work. By now the patron has probably sensed the tremendous amount of work that goes into a published genealogy, and perhaps at this point, she or he would like to have the name of a qualified genealogist who would be willing to do this work.

Genealogy became a profession with the establishment of a Board of Certification of Genealogists, which maintains standards and a code of ethics for those who wish to be certified as professional genealogists. The Board publishes an annual list of certified genealogists and record searchers. The list may be obtained for a nominal fee from the Board for Certification of Genealogists, Box 19165, Washington, D.C. 20036. The Association of Professional Genealogists in Salt Lake City, Utah, also publishes its own membership directory.

Another source for locating professional genealogists is *Who's Who in Genealogy and Heraldry*. The librarian can also direct a patron to other people working on the same family lines by referring him or her to notices in genealogical periodicals and directories.

SELECTED BIBLIOGRAPHY

Biography and Genealogy Master Index. Detroit: Gale, 1980– .

Bridger, Charles. *An Index to Printed Pedigrees*. Baltimore: Genealogical Publishing, 1969.

Catalogue of Genealogical and Historical Works: Library of the National Society of the Daughters of the American Revolution. Washington, D.C.: Memorial Continental Hall, 1940.

Church of Jesus Christ of Latter-day Saints. Genealogical Department. *International Genealogical Library Catalog: Surname Catalog (Microfiche)*. Salt Lake City: The Library, 1981– .

———. *Microfilm Card Catalog: Family History*. Salt Lake City: The Library, 1974.

Durrie, Daniel S. *Bibliographia Genealogica Americana: An Alphabetical Index to American Genealogies and Pedigrees Contained in State, County, and Town*

Histories, Printed Genealogies, and Kindred Works. Albany, N.Y.: Munsell, 1868–1908.

Filby, P. William, comp. *American and British Genealogy and Heraldry: A Selected List of Books.* 2nd ed. Chicago: ALA, 1975.

Genealogies and Family Histories—A Catalog of Demand Reprints. Ann Arbor, Mich.: University Microfilms, current ed.

The Grafton Index of Books and Magazine Articles on History, Genealogy, and Biography Printed in the United States on American Subjects During the Year 1909. New York: 1910.

Guide to Reprints: An International Bibliography of Scholarly Reprints. Kent, Conn.: Guide to Reprints, 1986.

Harvey, Richard. *Genealogy for Librarians.* London: Bingley, 1983.

Jacobus, Donald Lines. *Index to Genealogical Periodicals.* New Haven: Jacobus, 1932; Baltimore: Genealogical Publishing, 1981.

Kaminkow, Marion J., ed. *A Complement to Genealogies in the Library of Congress: A Bibliography.* Baltimore: Magna Carta, 1981.

Leidy, W. Phillip. *A Popular Guide to Government Publications.* 4th ed. New York: Columbia Univ. Pr., 1976.

Mayfield, David M. "The Genealogical Library of the Church of Jesus Christ of Latter-day Saints." *Library Trends* 32: 111–27 (Summer 1983).

Meyer, Mary Keysor, and P. William Filby, eds. *Who's Who in Genealogy and Heraldry.* Detroit: Gale, 1981.

Munsell's Genealogical Index. South Norwalk, Conn.: 1933– .

Parker, J. Carlyle. *Library Service for Genealogists.* Gale Genealogy and Local History Series, v.15. Detroit: Gale, 1981.

Schreiner-Yantis, Netti. *Genealogical Books in Print: A Catalogue of In-Print Titles, Useful and Interesting to Those Doing Genealogical Research.* Springfield, Va.: Schreiner-Yantis, 1981.

Sperry, Kip. *A Survey of American Genealogical Periodicals and Periodical Indexes.* Gale Genealogical and Local History Series, v.3. Detroit: Gale, 1978.

U.S. Library of Congress. *American and English Genealogies in the Library of Congress.* Baltimore: Genealogical Publishing, 1919, 1967.

———. *Genealogies in the Library of Congress: A Bibliography.* Baltimore: Magna Carta, 1972.

———. ———. Supplement, 1972–76. Baltimore: Magna Carta, 1977.

Chapter 2

Genealogical Research and Organization of Data

The librarian is expected, at the very least, to be able to recommend a good "how to" book to assist the beginning genealogist in his or her search. One could begin with either a basic book on historical research or a basic book on genealogical research.

HISTORICAL RESEARCH

Genealogical research is a form of historical research. Historical research can be defined as the application of a scientific method — beginning with the known and working toward the unknown — to the description and analysis of past events. Although an historian must depend on the observations and records of others, he or she must learn to evaluate those works before reaching conclusions. Authenticity of the records and their relevance to the subject being researched must be uppermost in the historian's mind as he or she studies both primary and secondary sources.

How to Do Research

Robert Shafer and other members of the Department of History at Syracuse University have edited *A Guide to Historical Method*, aimed primarily at beginning researchers in history. In his book *A Student's Guide to History*, Jule Benjamin includes a section on how to research family history. Frick's work *Library Research Guide to History* emphasizes library research in history.

Felt's *Researching, Writing, and Publishing Local History* may be used throughout the genealogical research project for information on research and organization. Divided into three sections, it focuses on researching in all types of sources, the mechanics of note taking and writing, and publishing a finished product.

General "How to" Books

Because so many books have been written on the subject of genealogical research, recommending handbooks and manuals is not as simple a task as it may appear. Lists from which to choose selected titles may be found in Parker's *Library Service for Genealogists*, which is Volume 15 in the Gale Genealogy and Local History Series, and Filby's *American and British Genealogy and Heraldry: A Selected List of Books*. For more recent titles, the librarian may choose from the most recent subject listing of *Books in Print* or from Schreiner-Yantis' *Genealogical Books in Print*.

In the past few years, many of the old standard "how to" books have been revised and new ones have been written, reflecting the expanding interest in genealogy. The authors of these works fall primarily into two categories—historians and genealogists—but the material covered is basically the same. Some of the books focus on a specific group of people or on a geographical location. Others are written for the advanced genealogist and should be recommended only after a basic book has been consulted.

The librarian can hardly go wrong in recommending one of the old standards that has withstood the test of time, in conjunction with one of the new books containing a strong chapter on the area being researched. Almost all libraries need more than one "how to" book, so care should be taken to choose those that cover different aspects of the genealogical research process.

Doane's *Searching for Your Ancestors*, Everton's *Handy Book for Genealogists*, Jacobus' *Genealogy as Pastime and Profession*, and Williams' *Know Your Ancestors* have undergone numerous revisions. Doane's classic book provides a very readable introduction to genealogy. It is based on his vast experience in researching New England sources and is, therefore, slanted toward that geographical area. Revisions have kept it up to date and enlarged its scope to include research outside the United States. Everton's book, a guide to state and county histories, maps, libraries, and other resources, is broader in geographical coverage than Doane's work. Jacobus has been called the "dean" of American genealogy by other genealogists. His book is a collection of his articles and may benefit both beginners and advanced researchers. Williams' book, compiled from her teaching experience in genealogy, is recommended for beginners as well as advanced researchers and focuses on the Midwest.

Some of the very helpful new books that have been written are Beard's *How to Find Your Family Roots*, Croom's *Unpuzzling Your Past*, Helmbold's *Tracing Your Ancestry*, Kirkham's *Research in American Genealogy*, Linder's *How to Trace Your Family History*, Stryker-Rodda's *How to Climb Your Family Tree*, and Lightman's *Your Family History*.

Beard's thick volume is divided into four parts. The first part is the "how to" section. The other parts are devoted to extensive bibliographies, including basic sources, state sources, and sources available for overseas searching. Croom's book contains an excellent chapter on family records, as well as record-keeping tips and genealogical charts.

The major strengths of Helbold's book are its genealogical charts and record-keeping tips. A separate *Logbook* contains useful reproducible forms and charts. Kirkham's basic "how to" book gives excellent general coverage of American genealogy. She also has written many specialized books on various aspects of genealogical research.

Linder's *How to Trace Your Family History* and Stryker-Rodda's *How to Climb Your Family Tree* cover the basics of research into family and public records, including information on using the library. Lightman, an historian, covers the subject of family history within the larger context of American history. His chapter on local history sources is outstanding.

A number of college level texts and reference books for serious students of genealogy also have been written. Wright's *Building an American Pedigree*, Jones' *Family History for Fun and Profit*, and Stevenson's *Search and Research* all are detailed surveys of genealogical sources.

Greenwood's *The Researcher's Guide to American Genealogy* is a comprehensive guide to the records used in American genealogical research. The American Society of Genealogist's *Genealogical Research: Methods and Sources*, sometimes used as a textbook, is another excellent guide to records and their use.

The Source, written for advanced genealogists by the country's leading genealogists, was one of the winners of the 1984 Best Reference Books Award. It identifies, locates, and interprets materials from the beginnings of the European colonization of America to 1910.

"How to" Books for Specific Ethnic Groups

Perhaps inspired by Alex Haley's *Roots*, "how to" ethnic genealogy books reflect a significant trend in genealogical publishing. These books are designed to deal with the special problems encountered by blacks and other groups. Westin's *Finding Your Roots* is helpful for people of various ethnic backgrounds, as is the more recent book *Ethnic Genealogy*, edited by Jessie Carney Smith. Black families may be assisted further by Blockson's *Black Genealogy* and Rose's *Black Genesis*.

The search for Native American roots can be assisted by such works as Blankenship's *Cherokee Roots*, *Our Native Americans: Their Records of Genealogical Value*, and Briton's *Library of Aboriginal American Literature*. Special problems of Jewish genealogy are addressed by Kurzweil's *From Generation to Generation* and Rottenberg's *Finding Our Fathers: A Guidebook to Jewish Genealogy*. Glynn's *Manual for Irish Genealogy*, Ryskamp's *Tracing Your Hispanic Heritage*, and Hinshaw's *The Encyclopedia of American Quaker Genealogy* address the special problems of researching other particular ethnic groups.

THE RESEARCH PROCESS

Genealogical research progresses in reverse chronology from the present to as far back as possible in the past, or beginning with the known and working toward the unknown. All along the way, the history and geography of the region of the family home are combined with the topical study of the family itself, bringing flesh to bare bones and making history come alive. To accomplish this feat, a variety of materials must be used, interpreted, and documented.

The research process for genealogy is not unlike the research process for the traditional term paper or professional paper, with which the librarian is quite familiar. Cown and McPherson's *Plain English Rhetoric and Reader*, used as an undergraduate text, is helpful as a reference on the research process. An easily accessible filing system must also be devised. Exact details, including names, dates, and other pertinent data, must be faithfully recorded. Burns' book *A System for Keeping Genealogical Research Records* is written especially for genealogical research.

Documents that can substantiate ancestry (birth certificates, marriage announcements, etc.) should be photocopied and kept with textual notes. The genealogist should pursue only one question (or one family line) at a time to avoid becoming hopelessly bogged down in what could become a trivial pursuit.

Note Taking

While reading, the genealogist should take notes on all the information needed. If the notes are not good enough, the genealogist can refer back to the source for additional information. This, however, should be avoided, if possible, because of the obvious waste of time involved.

The traditional way of taking notes is on 3″ × 5″ or 6″ × 8″ cards filed alphabetically in a box by a subject heading written at the top of the card. Some genealogists prefer notes written on loose pages and filed with photocopies of documents found during the research process. Whether notebooks or cards are used for recording notes, the following procedures are recommended: (1) keep notes brief but accurate; (2) put information into the researcher's own words or enclose in quotation marks more than three consecutive words taken from somebody else; and (3) record the *exact* source.

Stryker-Rodda includes a useful section on note taking in *How to Climb Your Family Tree: Genealogy for Beginners*. The novice would be well advised to photocopy whenever possible or to take complete notes with specific documentation to avoid backtracking.

Analyzing Data

Analysis of the data begins when the researcher starts taking notes, and it continues throughout the research process. All along the way, the researcher must decide what sources are pertinent to the research and which provide reliable true information.

Shafer and others describe three elements involved in analyzing historical data: external criticism, internal criticism, and synthesis. External criticism means determining a source's authorship and date. Although the beginning researcher will probably have little reason to question the authorship and date of sources discovered, he or she should develop the habit of thinking critically while gathering this information. The genealogist will probably be more concerned than will the beginning researcher with what historians call internal criticism, a method that helps determine a document's authenticity by appraising its consistency of language.

The third element involved in analyzing historical data is synthesis, or the blending of evidence into a defensible interpretation of historical events. This requires objectivity on the part of the researcher. It can be very tempting for a genealogist, eager to prove impressive family ties, to gloss over unpalatable facts, or even to invent facts in lieu of having complete information. Personal biases may influence the choice of words used in describing the past, giving a subjective slant to what is reported.

Organization of Material

After the notes have been taken and the data analyzed, the information gleaned must be organized. Most of the "how to" books on genealogy contain information on arranging the data into notebooks or onto pedigree charts. Some even give illustrations of charts properly filled in. As previously noted, Helmbold's *Logbook* is composed of genealogical charts and other forms that can be copied. Charts can also be purchased through genealogical societies, large genealogical libraries, or bookstores. One can also devise one's own chart or charts. The example shown in figure 2 is perhaps the least complicated for the novice genealogist to devise and contains spaces for the names and dates connected with the birth, death, and marriage of family members, beginning with one individual and working backward.

Doane writes that pedigree blanks form only a skeleton and that complete details of each family line should be written in paragraph form, with references given for full documentation. That is, indeed, the way a published genealogy should be arranged. In his chapter "How to Arrange a Genealogy," Doane tells how to number the generations, how to structure each paragraph, how to list pertinent information about any children, and how to write genealogical references.

Subject-specific software is being produced so microcomputers can be used to organize, store, and disseminate the names, vital data, etc., that are the results of genealogical research and, thus, to produce the finished family history. Many genealogy patrons already own personal computers. As microcomputers become more available to the public in libraries, librarians will be playing an even broader role in assisting the genealogy patron.

Toward this end, the librarian and patron would benefit from *Genealogy and Computers*, the proceedings of the July 1985 Genealogy Committee program (ALA Reference and Adult Services Division, History Section), Clement's *Genealogical Research Using Microcomputers*, Posey's *Tracing Your Roots by Computer*, and *Computer Genealogy* by Andereck and Pence. Several periodicals on geneal-

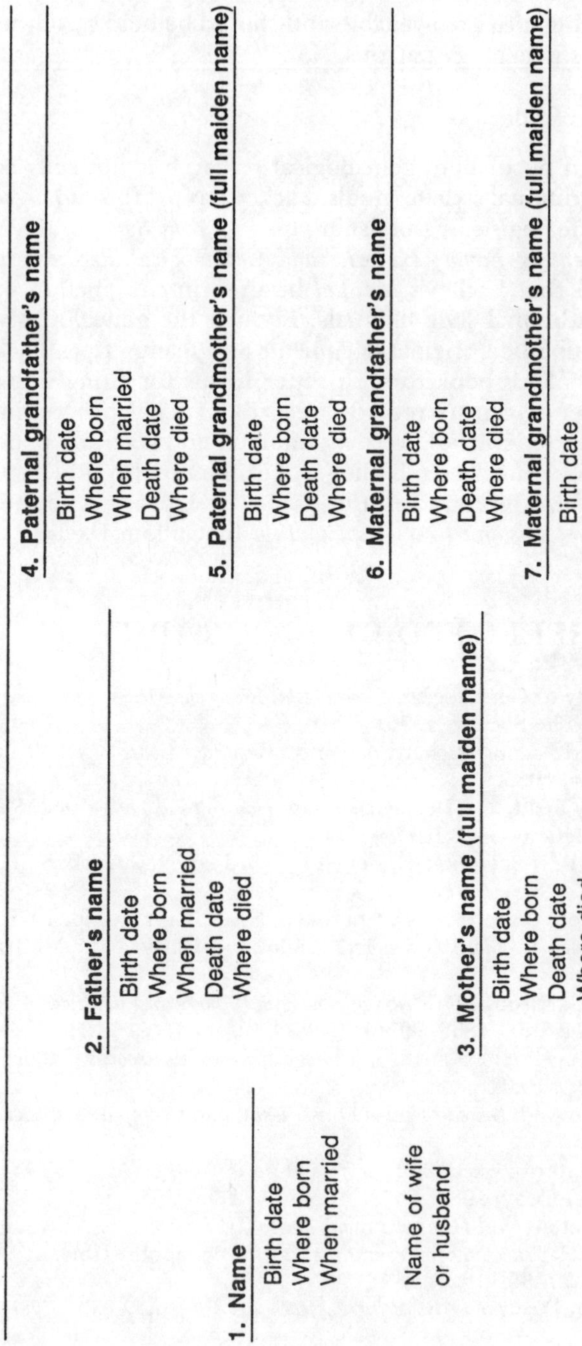

4. Paternal grandfather's name

Birth date
Where born
When married
Death date
Where died

5. Paternal grandmother's name (full maiden name)

Birth date
Where born
Death date
Where died

6. Maternal grandfather's name

Birth date
Where born
Death date
Where died

7. Maternal grandmother's name (full maiden name)

Birth date
Where born
Death date
Where died

2. Father's name

Birth date
Where born
When married
Death date
Where died

1. Name

Birth date
Where born
When married

Name of wife
or husband

3. Mother's name (full maiden name)

Birth date
Where born
Death date
Where died

Figure 2. An Example of a Genealogical Chart.

ogical computing also are available and should be held by libraries serving serious genealogy patrons.

Bibliographic Style

Documentation peculiar to genealogical research is not fully covered in the traditional style manuals. Lackey has performed a great service for genealogists by publishing his *Cite Your Sources: A Manual for Documenting Family Histories and Genealogical Records*. It is recommended that Lackey's *Manual* be used in conjunction with one of the traditional style manuals. Because the genealogist will use many unpublished original documents and manuscripts, Lackey devotes much of his book to the proper forms for citing unpublished documents, census records, records of legal proceedings, church records, federal land records, military and veterans' benefit records, and oral interviews. Bibliographic notation for oral history research may also be found in the American Library Association publication *Oral History: From Tape to Type* by Cullom Davis.

SELECTED BIBLIOGRAPHY

American Society of Genealogists. *Genealogical Research: Methods and Sources*. Washington: The Society, 1976.

Andereck, David A., and Richard A. Pence. *Computer Genealogy*. Salt Lake City: Ancestry, 1985.

Beard, Timothy Field, and Denise Demong. *How to Find Your Family Roots*. New York: McGraw-Hill, 1977.

Benjamin, Jule R. *A Student's Guide to History*. 3rd ed. New York: St. Martin's, 1983.

Blankenship, Bob. *Cherokee Roots*. Cherokee, N.C.: Blankenship, 1978.

Blockson, Charles L. *Black Genealogy*. Englewood Cliffs, N.J.: McGraw-Hill, 1977.

Briton, Daniel Garrison, ed. *Library of Aboriginal American Literature*. 4 vols. Philadelphia: Briton, 1882–90.

Burns, Louis. *A System for Keeping Genealogical Research Records*. Fallbrook, Calif.: Ciga Pr., 1982.

Clement, Charles, ed. *Genealogical Research Using Microcomputers*. Chicago: ALA, 1986.

Croom, Emily Anne. *Unpuzzling Your Past; A Basic Guide to Genealogy*. White Hall, Va.: Betterway, 1983.

Davis, Cullom, et al. *Oral History: From Tape to Type*. Chicago: ALA, 1977.

Doane, Gilbert H. *Searching for Your Ancestors*. Minneapolis: Univ. of Minnesota Pr., 1937–80.

Everton, George B. *Handy Book for Genealogists*. Logan, Utah: Everton, 1985.

Felt, Thomas E. *Researching, Writing, and Publishing Local History.* Nashville: Amer. Assn. for State and Local History, 1981.

Filby, P. William. *American and British Genealogy and Heraldry: A Selected List of Books.* Boston: New England Historic Genealogical Soc., 1983.

Frick, Elizabeth. *Library Research Guide to History: Illustrated Search Strategy and Sources.* Ann Arbor: Pierian Pr., 1980.

Genealogy and Computers. Chicago: ALA, 1986.

Glynn, Joseph Martin, Jr. *Manual for Irish Genealogy: A Guide to Methods and Sources for Tracing Irish Ancestry.* Newton, Mass.: The Irish Family History Soc., 1979.

Greenwood, Val D. *The Researcher's Guide to American Genealogy.* Baltimore: Genealogical Publishing, 1973.

Haley, Alex. *Roots: The Saga of an American Family.* New York: Doubleday, 1976.

Helmbold, F. Wilbur. *Tracing Your Ancestry, and Logbook.* Birmingham: Oxmoor, 1976.

Hinshaw, William. *The Encyclopedia of American Quaker Genealogy.* Baltimore: Genealogical Publishing, 1969–77.

Jacobus, Donald Lines. *Genealogy as Pastime and Profession.* Baltimore: Genealogical Publishing, 1930, 1968.

Jones, Vincent L., et al. *Family History for Fun and Profit.* Rev. ed. Salt Lake City: Genealogical Institute, 1972.

Kirkham, E. Kay. *Research in American Genealogy.* Salt Lake City: Deseret, 1962.

Kurzweil, Arthur. *From Generation to Generation.* New York: Schocken, 1982.

Lackey, Richard S. *Cite Your Sources; A Manual for Documenting Family Histories and Genealogical Records.* New Orleans: Polyanthos, 1980.

Lightman, Allan J. *Your Family History; How to Use Oral History, Personal Family Archives, and Public Documents to Discover Your Heritage.* New York: Vintage, 1978.

Linder, Bill R. *How to Trace Your Family History.* New York: Everest, 1978.

Our Native Americans: Their Records of Genealogical Value. Logan, Utah: Everton, 1980.

Posey, Joanna D. *Tracing Your Roots by Computer.* Orem, Utah: Posey Internatl., 1984.

Rose, James, and Alice Eichholz. *Black Genesis.* Detroit: Gale, 1978.

Rottenberg, Dan. *Finding Our Fathers: A Guidebook to Jewish Genealogy.* New York: Random, 1977.

Ryskamp, George R. *Tracing Your Hispanic Heritage.* Riverside, Calif.: Hispanic Family History Research, 1984.

Schreiner-Yantis, Netti. *Genealogical Books in Print: A Catalogue of In-Print Titles, Useful and Interesting to Those Doing Genealogical Research.* Springfield, Va.: Schreiner-Yantis, 1975, 1981.

Shafer, Robert Jones, et al., eds. *A Guide to Historical Method.* Homewood, Ill.: Dorsey Pr., 1974, 1980.

Smith, Jessie Carney, ed. *Ethnic Genealogy; A Research Guide.* Westport, Conn.: Greenwood, 1983.

The Source: A Guidebook of American Genealogy. Salt Lake City: Ancestry, 1984.
Stevenson, Noel C. *Search and Research.* Salt Lake City: Deseret, 1977.
Stryker-Rodda, Harriet. *How to Climb Your Family Tree; Genealogy for Beginners.* New York and Philadelphia: Lippincott, 1977.
Westin, Jeane Eddy. *Finding Your Roots.* New York: Ballantine, 1978.
Williams, Ethel W. *Know Your Ancestors.* Rutland, Vt.: Charles Tuttle, 1974.
Wright, Norman Edgar. *Building an American Pedigree.* Provo, Utah: Brigham Young Univ. Pr., 1974.

Chapter 3

Primary Sources

At various points in the research process, all genealogical researchers must assemble data from primary records. Even
those who have located published genealogies must link the immediate family members with the ancestors in the genealogy. Primary records are especially important for identifying ancestors and
for giving the basic facts about them.

Original, or primary, records are those written by either a par-
ticipant or an observer of an event at the time the event occurred.
In addition to records of births, marriages, and deaths, primary
records may be manuscripts, diaries, and old letters. They may
exist in unwritten form as oral histories or family photographs. It
is not difficult to see why primary records are preferred in genealogical research, for they are actual artifacts from the past,
whereas secondary sources are based on those artifacts.

Greenwood's *The Researcher's Guide to American Genealogy* and the
reference book titled *The Source* provide detailed instructions on
how to interpret various primary source materials. Wright's book
Building an American Pedigree contains photocopies of the records
a genealogist will consult, plus maps and bibliographies. The Library of Congress publication *National Union Catalog of Manuscript
Collections* reports collections of various types of primary materials
located in repositories around the country. Indexes identify the
material by subject, name, and place.

ORAL HISTORY

One of the most important methods of collecting genealogical information is through oral history, that is, by word of mouth. Older

19

relatives or other people can often provide information vital to a search that cannot be found recorded in family or other traditional records. If special care is taken in selecting the interviewee, conducting the interview, and processing the resulting information, oral history can be used to great advantage by the genealogist.

Oral history is recognized by the scholarly community as a method of gathering and preserving historical information in spoken form. The Oral History Association has set guidelines for the creation of authentic and reliable, as well as useful, source material. These guidelines were published by the Association in a booklet titled *Oral History Evaluation Guidelines*. Essentially, the guidelines state that interviews should be conducted with objectivity and integrity and that confidentiality should be maintained in areas stipulated by the interviewee.

Processing guidelines for the oral history tape or transcript are also given in *Oral History Evaluation Guidelines*. For example, time, place, subject, and other pertinent information must be recorded. Biographical information about the interviewees should also be given. Davis' *Oral History: From Tape to Type* deals with the special problems of writing and bibliographic notation based on the spoken word.

FAMILY RECORDS

Information relating to the birth, marriage, and death of individual family members makes up the "bare bones" of genealogical research. Additional information about the family members and their times enlivens history and makes the research more interesting.

How to Evaluate Records

After the family lineage chart is as complete as the researcher can make it, she or he should hand it over to older relatives for additions and corrections. The researcher also should conduct oral interviews at this time. The new information obtained can be checked for accuracy among the family papers one might find in attics and basements. Certificates of birth, marriage, and death are the most authoritative sources of information on vital life stages, and should be obtained for as many family members as possible. If there are no such certificates, other family papers will have to be consulted, but the kind of papers a researcher might expect to find will be determined by a family's record-keeping habits. How to glean information from such papers is discussed by Lightman in *Your Family History*, which would be useful to consult at this point in the research process.

For generations, almost all families have passed down the old family Bible with its pressed flowers and locks of hair hidden among the leaves, and its old, ornate handwritten notations of births, marriages, and deaths. Outside of a published genealogy, the most specific names and dates can be found there. Information from the family Bible is accepted as valid data in the field of genealogy if no other record can be found and if the entries have not been tampered with.[1] Differences in handwriting and ink are clues as to whether the entries were written at the time the events occurred or whether they were written by one person from memory at one sitting.

Diaries and old letters should be read as primary materials, for they contain not only information on vital family events, but they also evoke the times in which they were written. Descriptions of places and events may be presented more vividly in them than in any other historical record because of the writer's interest in and enthusiasm for the subject and because the event was recorded at the time it occurred. Something of the writer's personality may also be noted, for people often reveal themselves in their writings. The handwriting itself may be very ornate and somewhat difficult to read, especially if the script is different from what we use today. The beginner can gain valuable insight into the problem of handwriting from Kirkham's book *Handwriting of American Records for a Period of 300 Years*.

Deeds, account books, insurance policies, photographs, and wills are less important as records, but they should not be overlooked. The deed to a piece of property might provide a sufficient clue as to when a family migrated from one state to another, or even from one county to another. The person from whom the land was bought, whose name must appear on the deed, could be the best source of information outside the family on a certain relative. Account books are a running historical and economic record of the times. Insurance policies may be used to establish names and dates. Information written on the back of photographs, and even objects in the photographs themselves, identify names, dates, and places. Wills give names of spouses and children, and quite often indicate the eldest and youngest of the children.

---

1. Gilbert Harry Doane, *Searching for Your Ancestors* (Minneapolis: Univ. of Minnesota Pr., 1948), p.31.

Doane warns that the inexperienced genealogist should carefully study all available family records before he or she accepts as fact everything he or she may find written there. For example, relationships expressed in very old documents could be misleading. "Brother" and "sister" may refer to church friends or to in-laws, as well as to step-, half-, or blood-brothers and sisters. "Cousin" may be used to express any relationship, and "Mrs." used to be a title given to any female in her twenties, whether married or not.

What's in a Family Name?

Children often are named for their mothers or fathers or maybe even for ancestors that go several generations back. Therefore, a John Smith or a Jane Doe may appear in different generations. Repeated names are confusing at best and difficult to sort out if the research is not well documented and kept within the proper place and timeframe.

Children may also be given names reflecting the family's culture or lifestyle, such as "Faith" or "Hope" for families with a religious bent. Stewart's *American Given Names* gives the origins and meanings of names, including trends and regional and cultural influences on the naming of children. Family names also are subject to trends in culture and in the trades. Long's *Personal and Family Names* explains how family traditions, lifestyles, and occupations influence both the first and last names of people from many different areas.

The most difficult problem encountered in family research is finding out the original name of an adopted family member. In recent years papers for children given up for adoption have been sealed and are very difficult or impossible to examine. Conversely, early adoptions were very lax, and often no papers were filed at all.

It is possible that a court order could be obtained to unseal the records of an adoption. The adopted person might also be able to appeal to any number of people who might have been involved in the adoption. Papers concerning the event may be housed in a hospital, in the court where the adoption took place, at the agency that arranged the adoption, in the office of the lawyer who handled the case, or in the office of the doctor who delivered the baby. An adopted person who wants to find his or her natural parents can contact ALMA (Adoptees Liberty Movement Association) to learn the location of the nearest chapter. This special problem of names, as well as that of people who voluntarily changed their names, is addressed in Bander's *Change of Name and Law of Names,* Askin's

Search: A Handbook for Adoptees and Birthparents, and Triseliotes' *In Search of Origins—The Experiences of Adopted People.* Askin's book includes case studies and the addresses of help groups and agencies.

LOCAL PUBLIC RECORDS

The records found in a county courthouse or city hall are arranged more systematically than most family records, but they can be very time consuming to check, because many of them lack indexes. If the problem that needs to be solved through the use of public records can be solved without extensive searching, a clerk may perform this service and sometimes even mail the results. *Sheriffs and Clerks Directory* provides useful names and addresses, and *American County Government* by John Bollens is helpful in determining which county office can be expected to house particular records. H. G. Jones' book *Local Government Records: An Introduction to Their Management, Preservation, and Use* identifies various types of local records and explains their applications to historical research. The American Association for State and Local History, located in Nashville, Tennessee, has published a number of books and booklets on researching local history.

The Courthouse

Many of the local public records needed for genealogical research in the county courthouse are housed in the office of the chancery clerk. Records of wills and deeds, for instance, are indexed for quick reference. Family names and relationships can be obtained from records of wills, and the date on which the will was probated may help establish the death date of an individual. Land deeds will identify exactly where a relative lived, as well as the names of the buyers and sellers.

Tax records on private property may also be used to glean genealogical information. These are usually housed in the office of the tax assessor and/or collector.

Marriage records are housed in the office of the circuit clerk. These records will go back to about the time the county was organized, whereas state records of marriages may start much later. To examine marriage records, it is best to visit the courthouse or city hall in the county or city where the marriage took place. Other information, such as parentage and birth dates, can sometimes be obtained from the marriage record.

County Boundaries

Boundaries of counties were changed many times during the colonial period and during the early days of independence. For example, the 1830 census of the Michigan Territory lists an "Iowa County," which now is not in the state of Michigan at all.

If the county in which the town or village of the ancestral home was located is not known, Bowen's *The United States Post Office Guide* should be consulted in the library or at the post office. The *Guide* lists places alphabetically, giving the names of their counties. Another part of the *Guide*, "States and Counties," lists county seats, where courthouses are usually located.

Further research on the history of counties should be done if there appear to be discrepancies. County histories can be found in local history files in local public libraries, genealogical libraries, special collections departments of other types of libraries, or in state archives.

E. Kay Kirkham has written several useful books on genealogical research in counties and cities, including *Counties of the United States and Their Genealogical Value*; *A Genealogical and Historical Atlas of The United States of America*; *Handy Guide to Record Searching in the Larger Cities of the United States*; and *The Counties of the United States, Their Derivation and Census Schedules*. Everton's *Handy Book for Genealogists*, which is continually updated, contains state and county histories, maps, a list of libraries, information about where to write for records, and other helpful tips. Another genealogist, P. William Filby, has compiled *A Bibliography of American County Histories*. Written as an historical, rather than a genealogical tool, Kane's *The American Counties* is an excellent source to consult for county histories.

Cemeteries

To establish the date of death or even the date of birth of a family member, a trip to the cemetery may be in order. Headstones reveal birth and death dates, provided, of course, that the grave has been marked and that the inscription is still legible.

The exact wording on the stone must be recorded to obtain accurate information. For example, "consort" signifies that the husband or wife was living at the time of the spouse's death, whereas "wife" does not necessarily have that meaning. "Relict" always means widow (or widower), indicating that the wife survived her husband (or vice versa). It is best to photograph a headstone or to do a rubbing of it. A rubbing is made by covering the stone with light-weight paper and rubbing a wax crayon back and forth across the surface to reproduce the image found on the stone.

The outline of the history of a family or of an entire town can be inferred from the headstones. In the case of a tragic death, the reason for death is often recorded; or one can presume that if several members of a family died within a short time span, an epidemic or accident may have been the cause.

If the location or name of the cemetery is unknown, perhaps an index to names of cemeteries arranged by counties can be checked. These indexes are becoming quite prevalent in genealogical collections, special collections, and state archives, as members of the Daughters of the American Revolution and local genealogical society members are compiling them in earnest.

Community Groups

Cemetery records may be housed with church records, since cemeteries are often located alongside churches. Church records may also include baptisms and marriages performed in a particular church. Kirkham's *A Survey of American Church Records* details the types of records found in American churches of various denominations.

School records contain information about the student who was enrolled, as well as about the student's parents. These records are considered so reliable that their information can be used to obtain birth certificates, driver's licenses, and other records.

Personnel records or written reports of businesses may provide some personal information about individual family members. Likewise, Chamber of Commerce records and other civic and fraternal organization records may contain a variety of personal information.

From hospital records may be obtained birth or death information, as well as addresses, occupations, names, and relationships of various family members. The same types of information may be obtained from old city directories and telephone books.

STATE RECORDS

Records of births, deaths, marriages, and divorces not found locally may be obtained from state agencies, most of which began to compile records soon after a state's organization. State records are usually more recent than county records. Each state's Bureau of Vital Statistics (the actual name varies from state to state) also has its own rules, regulations, and fee structures for providing service.

The *National Directory of State Agencies* contains the addresses and telephone numbers, as well as the names and functions, of the different agencies within each state. Jones' *State Information Book* provides the same type of information found in the *National Directory*. It also lists the officers of major state services and of federal agencies located within a state. Several guides to vital records covering state and national levels have been written. For instance, the U.S. Department of Health and Human Services has published *Where to Write for Vital Records: Births, Deaths, Marriages, and Divorces;* the Consumer Education Research Center has published *Where to Write for Vital Records,* which includes forms for obtaining vital records; and Thomas Publications issues *Where to Write for Birth and Death, Marriage, Divorce Records in the United States Territories.*

The housing of state records follows the same pattern as that of national records. State records are housed at the various state agencies, as well as in the state archives in the state capitol, just as national records are housed at national agencies and in the National Archives.

Records that one can expect to find in the state archives include county histories, as previously noted, and compilations of some of the vital statistics records found in counties. Historical records of the state's government and supreme court are also housed in the state archives. War records containing the names and addresses of state citizens who served and pension records for Confederate veterans are housed there. State land grant records can be found in the state archives, as well as records for state-operated schools and orphanages. Genealogies of prominent families in the state may also be found there.

Both regular and special state censuses may be available. Some states had censuses taken regularly between the federal censuses. These censuses were first taken when a territory achieved statehood, but they were later abandoned in favor of the federal censuses. For example, Alabama took its first census in 1818 and its last in 1866, whereas Wyoming began its decennial census in 1895 and concluded it in 1925. The state census is a valuable tool for the genealogist because its schedules contain the names of individuals together with whatever information was included in the census inquiry. However, a state census may lack completeness and accuracy if it was taken by tax assessors.

Territorial censuses are mentioned in the multi-volume *Territorial Papers of the United States*. Details on state censuses and on some territorial censuses, and information on where they can be obtained are found in Dubester's book *State Censuses; An Annotated Bibliography of Censuses of Population Taken After the Year 1790 by States and Territories of the United States*. Individuals or institutions may obtain selected state censuses on loan or through purchase from the American Genealogical Lending Library.

FEDERAL RECORDS

The National Archives in Washington, D.C., houses all types of records pertaining to the federal government; it is the best place to look for records on the national level. Herman Viola's *The National Archives of the United States*, Meredith Colket's *Guide to Genealogical Records in the National Archives*, and the U.S. National Archives and Records Service's *Guide to Genealogical Research in the National Archives* explain in detail the types of records found in the archives.

The Census

One of the most important national records for genealogical research is the census population schedules. The schedules are also valuable records for establishing the legal age, citizenship, birthplace, and parentage of individuals. The information contained in the population census varies, becoming more detailed with time. Henry Dubester's *Catalog of United States Census Publications, 1790–1945* serves as a guide to census statistics and outlines the historical development of publication patterns.

The Bureau of the Census maintains nearly all of the original population schedules beginning with 1790. The first census of the United States comprised an enumeration of the people of the present states of Connecticut, Delaware, Georgia, Kentucky, Maine, Maryland, Massachusetts, New Hampshire, New Jersey, New York, North Carolina, Pennsylvania, Rhode Island, South Carolina, Tennessee, Vermont, and Virginia.

A complete set of the schedules for each state, with a summary for counties and in many cases for towns, was filed with the State Department, but, unfortunately, sets are not now complete. The returns for the states of Delaware, Georgia, Kentucky, New Jersey, Tennessee, and Virginia were destroyed when the British burned the Capitol in Washington during the War of 1812. For several of the states lacking schedules, it is likely that the Director of the Census can obtain lists of the names of almost all the heads of families at the date of the first census (U.S. Bureau of the Census, *Heads of Families at the First Census*).

The schedules of 1790 are excellent sources for the genealogist, since they give for each of the states covered a complete list of heads of families in the United States at the time the Constitution was adopted. Other family members were tallied by age, sex, and race. This practice continued through the census of 1840.

The 1850 census was the first to record each household member's name, age, occupation (if over 15 years of age), and place of birth. In the 1850 and 1860 censuses, slaves were counted in schedules, showing only their owner and the number of his slaves by age and sex.

The 1870 schedules indicate whether a parent of a person enumerated was foreign-born. The 1880 census includes the relationship of each individual to the head of the household. Beginning with the 1880 census, there is also a card index arranged by state or territory and the Soundex system, wherein names are arranged alphabetically by the first letter of the surname, then by a number representing the sound of the surname, and then alphabetically by given name (*Federal Population Censuses 1790–1890*).

Most of the 1890 population schedules were destroyed or badly damaged by a fire that broke out in the Commerce Department building in January 1921. Special schedules of the 1890 census were made enumerating Union Civil War veterans and widows of Union veterans. Additional assistance for the genealogist looking for Civil War ancestors may be found in Bertram Groene's *Tracing Your Civil War Ancestor*.

Microfilm copies of the original population schedules for 1790 to 1910 are available for sale by the National Archives and Records Service. (See appendix.) *Federal Population Censuses 1790–1890* and *The 1910 Federal Population Census* are catalogs published by the U.S. National Archives and Records Service from which one can order microfilm. The National Archives has also established a "Census Microfilm Rental Program" in Hyattsville, Maryland. A rental order must be placed through a local library or genealogical or historical association rather than by an individual. Microfilm copies also may be found in libraries, especially genealogy libraries and state and national archives. They may also be purchased or borrowed from the American Genealogical Lending Library in Bountiful, Utah.

Census indexes have been produced from the federal census for states or counties by individuals, societies, and computer companies. These indexes are simpler to use than the original population schedules, but they may contain errors.

Other National Records

The military records covering all branches of service from the Philippine Insurrection (1899–1902), the Spanish-American War (1898–99), the Indian Wars, the Civil War (1861–65), the Mexican-American War (1846–48), the War of 1812, and the Revolutionary War are on file in the National Archives in Washington, D.C., and in regional record offices throughout the country, as well as in the Veterans Administration and other national agencies. These records sometimes list places and dates of birth and death. Requests for copies of military records may be made by filling out a form and giving as much information as possible to Military Service Records, National Archives and Records Service.

Revolutionary War pension applications and other military records are available on microfilm from the American Genealogical Lending Library. In 1966, the National Genealogical Society published an *Index to Revolutionary War Pension Applications*, which should be available in genealogical and other lending libraries.

Records relating to veterans who applied for pensions or bounty land warrants are also available in the National Archives. The archive files hold pension applications from those who served in the army, navy, or marines between 1775 and 1916. The U.S. Congress' *Report from the Secretary of War in Relation to the Pension Establishment of the United States* gives a good overview of the pension system. A pension file contains, in addition to the application, documents submitted to support a claim. Large libraries may carry the *List of Pensioners on the Roll January 1, 1883*, published as Senate Executive Document 84, 47th Congress, 2nd Session and reprinted in 1970 by the Genealogical Publishing Company.

Those who served in the country's earliest wars, beginning with the Revolutionary War, were offered public land for their services. The land-grant files are similar to the pension files. Both usually show the veteran's name, rank, military unit, and period of service. Also housed in the National Archives are various other land records, such as homestead applications and private land claim files. In these files one can expect to find the applicant's name, location of land, address, date the land was acquired, and such vital information as age, date and place of birth, marital status, and perhaps facts about the applicant's family.

Some mortality schedules were kept from 1850 through 1900, recording deaths that occurred in the years between the censuses.

Information in the schedules includes name, age, sex, color, birthplace, and date and cause of death. By 1900, most states had established registrations of death, so the mortality schedules were no longer kept. Mortality records are kept in state archives and also on microfilm in the National Archives. The National Archives also maintains records of births, marriages, and deaths at army facilities from 1884 to 1912.

Naturalization records, in addition to showing age or date of birth, also indicate the nationality of those who applied for naturalization. Records for Washington, D.C., and a few states are kept in the National Archives. Passenger arrival lists, useful in identifying immigrant ancestors, are also located in the National Archives. An inventory of these lists can be found in Filby's *Passenger and Immigration Lists Index*.

SELECTED BIBLIOGRAPHY

Allaben, Frank, and Mabel Washburn. *How to Trace and Record Your Own Ancestry*. New York: The National Historical Co., 1932.

Askin, Jayne. *Search: A Handbook for Adoptees and Birthparents*. New York: Harper, 1982.

Bander, Edward J. *Change of Name and Law of Names*. Dobbs Ferry, N.Y.: Oceana, 1973.

Bollens, John C. *American County Government, with an Annotated Bibliography*. Beverly Hills, Calif.: Sage, 1969.

Bowen, Eli. *The United States Post Office Guide*. New York: Arno, 1976.

Colket, Meredith Bright. *Guide to Genealogical Records in the National Archives*. Washington, D.C.: National Archives and Records Service, 1964.

Davis, Cullom. *Oral History: From Tape to Type*. Chicago: ALA, 1977.

Dubester, Henry J. *Catalog of United States Census Publications, 1790–1945*. New York: Greenwood, 1968; B. Franklin, 1971.

Everton, George B. *Handy Book for Genealogists*. Logan, Utah: Everton, 1985.

Federal Population Censuses, 1790–1890; A Catalog of Microfilm Copies of the Schedules. Washington, D.C.: National Archives and Records Service, 1978.

Filby, P. William. *A Bibliography of American County Histories*. Baltimore: Genealogical Publishing, 1985.

———, and Mary K. Meyer. *Passenger and Immigration Lists Index*. Detroit: Gale, 1985.

Greenwood, Val D. *The Researcher's Guide to American Genealogy*. Baltimore: Genealogical Publishing, 1973.

Groene, Bertram Hawthorne. *Tracing Your Civil War Ancestor*. Winston-Salem, N.C.: John F. Blair, 1981.

Jones, Geraldine U., and Leonard P. Hirsch, eds. *State Information Book.* Vienna, Va.: Infax Corp., 1985.

Jones, H. G. *Local Government Records: An Introduction to Their Management, Preservation, and Use.* Nashville: Amer. Assn. for State and Local History, 1983.

Kane, Joseph Nathan. *The American Counties; Origins of County Names, Dates of Creation and Organization, Area, Population Including 1980 Census Figures, Historical Data, and Published Sources.* 4th ed. Metuchen, N.J.: Scarecrow, 1983.

Kirkham, E. Kay. *Counties of the United States and Their Genealogical Value.* Salt Lake City: Deseret, 1965.

——. *The Counties of the United States, Their Derivation and Census Schedules.* Salt Lake City: Kay Publishing, 1961.

——. *A Genealogical and Historical Atlas of the United States of America.* Logan, Utah: Everton, 1976.

——. *Handwriting of American Records for a Period of 300 Years.* Logan, Utah: Everton, 1973.

——. *Handy Guide to Record Searching in the Larger Cities of the United States.* Logan, Utah: Everton, 1974.

——. *A Survey of American Church Records: Major and Minor Denominations, Before 1880–90.* 4th rev. ed. Logan, Utah: Everton, 1978.

Lightman, Allan J. *Your Family History; How to Use Oral History, Personal Family Archives, and Public Documents to Discover Your Heritage.* New York: Vintage, 1978.

Long, Harry Alfred. *Personal and Family Names.* Detroit: Gale, 1968.

National Directory of State Agencies. Washington, D.C.: Information Resources Pr., 1984.

National Genealogical Society. *Index to Revolutionary War Pension Applications in the National Archives.* Washington, D.C.: The Society, 1976.

Oral History Evaluation Guidelines. n.p.: Oral History Assn., 1980.

Sheriffs and Clerks Directory. Miami: Sheriffs and Clerks Directory, 1983.

The Source: A Guidebook of American Genealogy. Salt Lake City: Ancestry, 1984.

Stewart, George R. *American Given Names: Their Origin and History in the Context of the English Language.* New York: Oxford Univ. Pr., 1979.

Territorial Papers of the United States. Washington, D.C.: Govt. Print. Off., 1934.

Triseliotes, John B. *In Search of Origins—The Experiences of Adopted People.* London: Routledge & Paul, 1973.

U.S. 23rd Congress. 1st Session. *Report from the Secretary of War in Relation to the Pension Establishment of the United States.* Baltimore: Genealogical Publishing, 1968.

U.S. 47th Congress. 2nd Session. *List of Pensioners on the Roll January 1, 1883.* Washington, D.C. and Baltimore: Genealogical Publishing, 1883, 1970.

U.S. Bureau of the Census. *Heads of Families at the First Census, 1790.* 12 vols. Washington, D.C.: Govt. Print. Off., 1907–9.

U.S. Department of Health and Human Services. *Where to Write for Vital Records: Births, Deaths, Marriages, and Divorces.* Hyattsville, Md.: Natl. Ctr. for Health Statistics, 1984.

U.S. National Archives and Records Service. *Guide to Genealogical Research in the National Archives.* Washington, D.C.: National Archives and Records Service, 1983.

———. *The 1910 Federal Population Census; A Catalog of Microfilm Copies of the Schedules.* Washington, D.C.: National Archives Trust Fund Board, 1982.

Viola, Herman J. *The National Archives of the United States.* New York: Abrams, 1984.

Where to Write for Birth and Death, Marriage, Divorce Records in the United States Territories. Los Angeles: Thomas Pubns., 1981.

Where to Write for Vital Records: Births, Deaths, Marriages, and Divorces; Including Forms for Obtaining These and Other Vital Records. South Orange, N.J.: Consumer Education Research Ctr., 1985.

Wright, Norman Edgar. *Building an American Pedigree.* Provo, Utah: Brigham Young Univ. Pr., 1974.

Chapter 4

Secondary Sources

References to secondary sources have been made throughout this book, underscoring the importance of these materials in genealogical research. Secondary sources can serve to fill gaps in primary records. Material based on primary sources that has been rearranged for a particular purpose or audience is secondary material. Secondary sources such as the indexes and guides used to get to the information in primary sources were discussed in the first chapter. Newspapers; biographical directories; directories of organizations; city directories; genealogical periodicals; county, state, and national histories; encyclopedias; almanacs; and handbooks are other examples of secondary sources. For those ancestors who have already been identified, secondary sources provide the background information about their lives needed to enrich the genealogy.

Most secondary source materials are purchased for broad library uses and may be found in most public and academic libraries. Some of the more specialized sources may be found only in genealogical or historical libraries.

NEWSPAPERS

Newspaper announcements of births, weddings, and deaths, or other events that affect families may be as accurate as primary records, because they are contemporaneous with the events. It is true that errors are made in newspaper reporting, but it is also true that errors are sometimes made in the transcribing of information found in primary documents.

Some newspapers run genealogical columns that provide information on particular families. Anita Milner names columns appearing in a variety of newspapers in her *Newspaper Genealogical Column Directory*. Watkins' book *Ancestor Hunting* contains reprints from such a column from the *Shreveport Journal* during the 1960s. Although published in Louisiana, names mentioned in the column are not restricted to Louisiana families.

Newspapers may be located in libraries of all types and in state and national archives. City and county papers may also be located in city halls, county courthouses, and newspaper offices. Sometimes clippings, brief indexes, or information about indexes may be found in a newspaper office. Most local and state newspapers are not indexed, so one would need to know at least the approximate publication date of the article she or he was seeking; otherwise she or he could spend many hours searching for it. Fortunately, this picture is changing, as individuals, companies, and genealogical and historical groups are taking on the job of indexing old newspapers.

The *New York Times* is the closest thing we have to a national newspaper. Indexed by subject, name, and organization in the *New York Times Index,* it covers the period from 1851 to the present. Because each entry includes a brief abstract of the news story, a single fact or date can be obtained from the index, enabling the researcher to locate information in other sources as well. All issues of the newspaper also are readily available on microfilm. Another large newspaper available on microfilm and at least partially indexed by the *Christian Science Monitor Index* is the *Christian Science Monitor*. The *Wall Street Journal* is indexed from 1959 by the *Wall Street Journal Index*. The *Chicago Tribune*, the *Los Angeles Times,* the *Times Picayune of New Orleans,* and the *Washington Post* are indexed from 1972 by the *Newspaper Index.*

A number of tools are useful for locating names of newspapers, publishing dates, and availability of back files. *Ayer Directory of Publications* and *Editor and Publisher* are continuously updated, providing the most current information about newspapers. Neither of these publications, however, indicates whether back issues of a newspaper are available or where to find them. Other finding aids include Brigham's *History and Bibliography of American Newspapers, 1690–1820,* Gregory's *American Newspapers, 1821–1936,* and the Library of Congress publication *Newspapers in Microform.* The latter source is perhaps the most helpful, because newspapers that have been microfilmed may often be borrowed through interlibrary loan.

COLLECTIVE BIOGRAPHY

Biographical works can be searched for ancestors whose names and possible occupations may be known either from oral family evidence or from previous research that yielded partial information. The works consulted can be considered authoritative if objective and accurate research has been conducted in collecting the biographical information. Such information typically is obtained in two different ways—from questionnaires submitted to the subjects or by consulting original sources. Biographies compiled from research into primary sources are recommended.

General collective biographies contain accounts of the lives of famous people. Subject biographies contain information on lesser-known individuals. Some career-type information must already be known about ancestors to search for them in subject biographies. One might wonder whether biographical information about famous or prominent individuals is useful to many researchers. Because researchers are more likely to be aware of a prominent individual in the family's past, however remote the relationship may be to the immediate, living family, important connections can be made that lead to vital information about other ancestors. Collective biographies usually list names of spouses, children, parents, places of residence, and educational institutions attended.

General Biography

Current Biography is the most popular of the current biographies found in most libraries. It is indexed by profession, as well as by name, and the articles are long enough to include all the important information about a person. *Who's Who in America, with World Notables,* which is updated constantly, contains high quality biographical information. *Webster's Biographical Dictionary* heavily emphasizes Americans and contains concise information on people of all periods.

Who Was Who in America is a compilation of biographies originally published in *Who's Who* of people now deceased, as are the *Dictionary of American Biography* and the *National Cyclopedia of American Biography.* Of course, persons represented by these sources must be well known. The *New York Times Obituaries Index, 1858–1968* includes summations of the lives of lesser-known persons and is not limited to Americans. It is continued by the *New York Times Biographical Edition: A Compilation of Current Biographical Information of General Interest.*

Subject Biography

Collective biographies exist for most career fields, many religious groups, and many political or special interest groups. Various professional fields are represented by the titles *Who's Who in American Politics, Taylor's Encyclopedia of Government Officials, Dictionary of American Scholars, Leaders in Education, American Men and Women of Science,* and many others. Greenwood Press has been very active in publishing collective subject biographies. Sample titles include Withey's *Biographical Dictionary of American Architects Deceased, Biographical Dictionary of American Educators, Biographical Dictionary of Business Leaders,* and *Dictionary of American Medical Biography.*

In recent years, a number of titles have been published by Greenwood Press and others that contain biographies of 18th- and 19th-century figures. Published in 1983, *American Writers Before 1800* contains information on many lesser-known early American writers and provides a chronology of the period. *Biographical Dictionary of American Labor,* published in 1984, has entries for 19th-century labor leaders. *American Blue-Book of Funeral Directors,* published in 1972, covers the post-Civil War period. Other diverse titles used for retrospective searching include the U.S. Congress' *Official Congressional Directory, Great Composers, 1300–1900, Composers Since 1900, American Authors: 1600–1900,* Groce's *Dictionary of Artists in America, 1564–1860,* and the Gale Research Company's *Dictionary of Literary Biography.*

Background for and biographical information about ancestors with known or suspected religious affiliations may be obtained from publications focused on different religious groups, such as Bodensieck's *Encyclopedia of the Lutheran Church,* published in 1965; the *Mennonite Encyclopedia,* published from 1955 to 1959; and Madison's *Eminent American Jews: 1776 to the Present,* published in 1970. Retrospective biographical searching among religious groups of various denominations may be conducted with Sprague's *Annals of the American Pulpit.* People of known denominational affiliation may be searched in the Methodist Episcopal Church's *Minutes of the Annual Conferences, 1773–1835,* Beecher's *Index of Presbyterian Ministers, Containing the Names of All the Ministers of the Presbyterian Church in the United States, 1706–1881,* American Catholic Historical Society of *Philadelphia Records,* and Lasher's *The Ministerial Directory of the Baptist Churches in the United States of America.*

The *Dictionary of American Military Biography,* published in 1984, covers the period from the French and Indian War to the Vietnam conflict, and includes names and brief biographies of soldiers from those wars. A listing in this source could provide necessary clues for further research into the war records housed in the National Archives. Other titles covering specific wars have been published, including Lossing's *Pictorial Fieldbook of the Revolution, Who Was Who During the American Revolution*, Dyer's *A Compendium of the War of the Rebellion*, Evans' *Confederate Military History*, and Ellet's *The Women of the American Revolution*.

Biographies useful for searching for outstanding women are *Notable American Women* and *Notable American Women, The Modern Period*. Particularly useful for 19th-century biography is Willard's *Women of the Century*.

Subject Encyclopedias

The International Encyclopedia of the Social Sciences has a detailed index and contains some 600 biographies of outstanding figures in anthropology, economics, geography, history, law, political science, psychology, sociology, and statistics. More useful for retrospective, historical material is the older *Encyclopedia of the Social Sciences*, which contains over 4,000 biographies.

Biographies are generally not found in encyclopedias in the pure and applied sciences, but they may be found in abundance in encyclopedias of the humanities. William Benét's *The Reader's Encyclopedia* is a comprehensive work that very briefly covers all the humanities of all nations and of all periods. More subject-specific encyclopedias in which articles about people can be found are the *Encyclopedia of World Art*, Baldwin's *Dictionary of Philosophy and Psychology*, Hastings' *Encyclopedia of Religion and Ethics*, Cassell's *Encyclopedia of Literature*, and Grove's *Dictionary of Music and Musicians*.

Directories of Organizations

The many thousands of clubs; institutions; associations; fraternal, professional, and business groups; and governmental organizations that exist are connected with individuals either through their staffs or through their memberships. Directories of organizational members or printed histories of organizations are useful to supplement biographical sources. Directories may be local, governmental, institutional, commercial, or professional. To locate the biography of a business person, for example, one could consult a general "who's who," a subject-oriented biography, the records of Dun and Bradstreet, or a specific business directory or printed history.

The *Encyclopedia of Associations* is probably the best known and most up-to-date tool for locating the names, addresses, and publications of different associations. The *Guide to American Directories*, arranged by subject and title, describes more than 3,350 directories of institutions, individuals, and businesses. Other guides to directories are Spear's *Bibliography of American Directories through 1860*, the *Directory of Historical Societies and Agencies, PAIS Bulletin, Business Reference Sources*, and the *Monthly Catalog of U.S. Government Publications*. The *World Almanac* and other almanacs also list associations and their addresses.

Names, addresses, and information on people and business firms may be found in old or current telephone directories and city directories. The latter are usually older than telephone directories. Clues to a family's history may be obtained by studying city directories over a period of years. For example, the first entry of a family name will probably indicate the date the family moved to the area. When the name no longer appears, the person either moved or died. It might then be possible, based on this lead, to locate an obituary. Having an exact address for the family will help in the search through other records, especially federal census records. The existence and location of city directories can be determined from *City Directories of the United States in Microform*.

Other local directories may be put out by schools in the form of yearbooks. Complete collections will probably be found in the individual schools. Clubs, business, and professional organizations may publish annual reports or annual membership directories. Some of these same groups may publish national or international directories. For example, *American Universities and Colleges* is a national school directory, as is Baird's *Manual of American College Fraternities*. Biographical sketches of alumni and recipients of honorary degrees from Harvard, Yale, Princeton, and Columbia are contained in Chamberlain's *Universities and Their Sons*. National directories exist for the professions, such as the *Martindale-Hubbell Law Directory* and the *Who's Who in Library and Information Services*, among many others.

Periodicals and Periodical Indexes

General information on genealogy and articles on various aspects of the subject, as well as good bibliographies, can be found in genealogical periodicals. As noted in Chapter 1, individual family genealogies may also be contained in these special periodicals. Some of the more useful genealogical periodicals are indexed in *Genealogical Periodical Annual Index*, the *American Genealogical-Biographical Index to American Genealogical, Biographical, and Local History Materials*, and Sperry's *Index to Genealogical Periodical Literature, 1960–*

77. *A Survey of American Genealogical Periodicals and Periodical Indexes* provides access points to genealogical periodical literature.

General periodicals and periodical indexes that cover a long time span may also be helpful to the genealogist in weaving the fabric of the historical background of a family. Dating from 1905, *The Readers' Guide to Periodical Literature* covers many periodicals and many subject fields. Its forerunner was *Poole's Index to Periodical Literature, 1802–1906*. The *Social Sciences and Humanities Index,* dating from 1916, is the second most important general index.

Several volumes, using various approaches, cover periodical literature in history. *Historical Abstracts* is divided into two sections, arranged chronologically. Part A, called "Modern History," covers the time span 1450–1914. Part B, called "Twentieth Century," covers 1914 to the present. The abstracts contain subject, geographical, and name indexes, and provide a concise way to survey the literature without having to look at all of the individual titles. *America: History and Life* is arranged in much the same way as *Historical Abstracts.*

Individual periodical titles with long runs published by scholarly bodies in the field of history may be consulted directly. The *William and Mary Quarterly,* published since 1892, the same year the Daughters of the American Revolution began publishing their *Magazine,* is national in scope and is concerned with early American history and culture. The *American Historical Review,* published by the American Historical Association, followed in 1895. The Organization of American Historians has published the *Journal of American History* since 1907; it was long published under the title *Mississippi Valley Historical Review.*

State-wide historical groups have also published periodicals for many years. For researchers seeking state histories, these periodicals are the best sources available, but they also may contain information of national interest. Two examples of such publications are *Florida Historical Quarterly,* published by the Florida Historical Society, and *South Carolina Historical Magazine,* published by the South Carolina Historical Society. The *Virginia Genealogist,* the *New York Genealogical and Biographical Record,* and *Kentucky Ancestors* are other journals valuable for researchers concerned with records of those states.

Recommended by P. William Filby for any library that serves genealogists, some of the most outstanding genealogy journals are the *Detroit Society for Genealogical Research Magazine, Genealogical Journal, Genealogist, National Genealogical Society Quarterly,* and the *Mayflower Quarterly.*

Geographical/Historical Sources

Old maps; atlases; and local, state, and national histories will give a picture of the background from which one's ancestors came, especially if they were written during the time the family lived in a particular area. Historical atlases are useful in genealogical research because the maps show adjustments in boundaries caused by historical events. Perhaps the most outstanding historical atlas is Shepherd's *Historical Atlas*. It first appeared in 1911 and has been frequently revised since then. Gilbert's *Recent History Atlas: 1870 to the Present Day* is said to be a continuation of Shepherd's work.

The 20-volume set *Annals of America* is a chronological record of American life from 1492 to the present, and it contains copies of thousands of original documents. It also has an alphabetical index. Carrying the study of American history into the twentieth century is Adams' *Dictionary of American History*. Its entries are organized by the major periods of American history, making it easy to use for quick reference. The companion to Adams' *Dictionary* is his *Album of American History*, which is indexed by event, subject, and name.

Many state histories can be located in even the smallest public libraries. Histories of towns and counties are also available in libraries and in archives collections. Such repositories will likely hold the state, county, and town histories that were inspired by the Centennial in 1876 and by the Bicentennial in 1976. In addition to establishing a locale's historical background, many state histories contain biographies and discussions of families prominent in the area. Peterson's *Consolidated Bibliography of County Histories in Fifty States in 1961* helps to locate biographies found in county histories.

Collective Family Histories

Researchers who have succeeded in tracing one or more family lines back to the colonial and early independence periods should check the older collective family histories. Virkus' *Abridged Compendium of American Genealogy* is a well-indexed encyclopedia of the "first families" of America. The introduction states that while not all families entitled to inclusion are represented in the list of "first families," practically every name distinguished in the early history of the country will be found. It includes 5,000 records and more than 7,000 lineages.

Historical societies have published several family histories. Among them are *American Families of Historic Lineage*, published from 1910 to 1919 by the National Americana Society; Sutter's *American Fam-*

ilies, Genealogical and Heraldic, published by the American Historical Society in 1900; and DuBin's *Five Hundred First Families of America,* published in several editions by the Historical Publication Society.

Because of the upsurge in interest in genealogy, the Genealogical Publishing Company is currently very active in publishing secondary sources compiled from primary records of all types. Any library actively serving genealogical researchers should have in its files the latest copy of the Genealogical Publishing Company's catalog, some of whose titles follow. *American Ancestry,* originally published in the late 1800s and reissued by the company, gives name and male descent of Americans whose ancestors settled in this country before the signing of the Declaration of Independence in 1776. First published in 1923 and reprinted numbers of times by the company, with the latest publication appearing in 1984, Frank Holmes' *Directory of the Ancestral Heads of New England Families, 1620–1700* is an alphabetical arrangement of approximately 15,000 families who arrived in New England during the 17th century. The company also has published Hotten's *The Original Lists of Persons of Quality, 1600–1700, Burke's Genealogical and Heraldic History of the Colonial Gentry, Burke's American Families with British Ancestry,* and many others.

Individual family histories, compiled and privately published by amateurs, may be only "twice told tales." Collected family histories may also contain errors, but, if published by a reputable firm and with some evidence of documentation present, they may be approached with confidence. When in doubt, the researcher should take the information in hand and seek proof from primary sources such as official records.

SELECTED BIBLIOGRAPHY

Adams, James T. *Album of American History.* New York: Scribner's, 1981.
——, ed. *Dictionary of American History.* New York: Scribner's, 1976–78.
America: History and Life. Santa Barbara, Calif.: ABC-Clio Information Services, 1964.
American Ancestry. Albany, N.Y.: Munsell, 1887–99.
American Authors: 1600–1900. New York: Wilson, 1938.
American Catholic Historical Society of Philadelphia Records. Philadelphia: The Society, 1886– .
American Families of Historic Lineage: Being a Genealogical, Historical, and Biographical Account of Representative Families of Eminent American and Foreign Ancestry. New York: Natl. Americana Soc., 1910–19.

American Genealogical-Biographical Index to American Genealogical, Biographical, and Local History Materials. Middletown, Conn.: 1952– .

American Genealogist. Warwick, R.I.: Ruth Wilder Sherman, 1922; Detroit: Gale, 1975.

American Historical Review. Washington, D.C.: Amer. Historical Assn., 1895–.

American Men and Women of Science: A Biographical Directory. New York: Bowker, 1972– .

American Universities and Colleges. Washington, D.C.: Amer. Council on Education, 1983.

American Writers Before 1800: A Biographical and Critical Dictionary. Westport, Conn.: Greenwood, 1983.

Annals of America. 20 vols. Chicago: Encyclopaedia Britannica, 1969.

Author Biographies Master Index. 2nd ed. Detroit: Gale, 1984.

Baird, William Raimond. *Manual of American College Fraternities.* Menasha, Wisc.: Banta, 1963.

Baldwin, James Mark. *Dictionary of Philosophy and Psychology.* New York: Macmillan, 1901–5.

Beecher, Willis Judson. *Index of Presbyterian Ministers, Containing the Names of All the Ministers of the Presbyterian Church in the United States, 1706–1881.* Philadelphia: Presbyterian Board of Pubns., 1883.

Benét, William Rose. *The Reader's Encyclopedia.* 2nd ed. New York: Crowell, 1965.

Biographical Dictionary of American Educators. Westport, Conn.: Greenwood, 1978.

Biographical Dictionary of American Labor. 2nd ed. Westport, Conn.: Greenwood, 1984.

Biographical Dictionary of Business Leaders. Westport, Conn.: Greenwood, 1983.

Bodensieck, Julius. *Encyclopedia of the Lutheran Church.* Minneapolis: Augsburg, 1965.

Brigham, Clarence S. *History and Bibliography of American Newspapers, 1690–1820.* Worcester, Mass.: Amer. Antiquarian Soc., 1947; Westport, Conn.: Greenwood, 1976.

Burke, John Bernard. *Burke's American Families with British Ancestry: The Lineages of 1,600 Families of British Origin Now Resident in the United States of America.* Baltimore: Genealogical Publishing, 1977.

———. *Burke's Genealogical and Heraldic History of the Colonial Gentry.* Baltimore: Genealogical Publishing, 1970.

Business Reference Sources. Boston: Harvard, 1971.

Cassell's Encyclopedia of Literature. London: Cassell, 1953.

Chamberlain, Joshua Lawrence. *Universities and Their Sons: History, Influence, and Characteristics of American Universities.* Boston: Herdon, 1898–1900.

Christian Science Monitor: Subject Index. Boston: Christian Science Monitor, 1960– .

City Directories of the United States in Microform. New Haven, Conn.: Research Publishers, 1980.

Composers Since 1900. New York: Wilson, 1969.

Cutter, William Richard. *American Families, Genealogical, and Heraldic.* New York: Amer. Historical Soc., 1900.

Daughters of the American Revolution Magazine. Washington, D.C.: Natl. Soc. of the Daughters of the Amer. Revolution, 1892– .

Detroit Society for Genealogical Research Magazine. Detroit: Detroit Soc. for Genealogical Research, 1937.

Dictionary of American Biography. New York: Scribner's, 1928–58.

Dictionary of American Medical Biography. Westport, Conn.: Greenwood, 1984.

Dictionary of American Military Biography. Westport, Conn.: Greenwood, 1984.

Dictionary of American Scholars. 5th ed. New York: Bowker, 1969.

Directory of Historical Societies and Agencies in the United States and Canada. 12th ed. Nashville: American Assn. for State and Local History, 1982.

DuBin, Alexander. *Five Hundred First Families of America.* New York: Historical Publication Soc., 1978.

Dyer, Frederick Henry. *A Compendium of the War of the Rebellion.* New York: Yoseloff, 1959.

Editor and Publisher. New York: Editor and Publisher, 1927– .

Ellet, Elizabeth F. *The Women of the American Revolution.* Williamstown, Mass.: Corner House, 1980.

Evans, Clement A. *Confederate Military History: A Library of Confederate States History.* Atlanta: Confederate Pubs., 1899; Atlanta: Blue and Gray Pr., 1975.

Florida Historical Quarterly. Gainesville: Florida Historical Soc., 1908– .

Gale Research Company. *Dictionary of Literary Biography.* Detroit: Gale, 1982.

Genealogical Journal. Salt Lake City: Genealogical Assn., 1972– .

Genealogical Periodical Annual Index, 1981. Bowie, Md.: Heritage, 1985.

Genealogist. New York: Assn. for the Promotion of Scholarship in Genealogy, 1980.

Gilbert, Martin. *Recent History Atlas: 1870 to the Present Day.* New York: Macmillan, 1966.

Great Composers, 1300–1900. New York: Wilson, 1966.

Gregory, Winifred. *American Newspapers, 1821–1936.* Millwood, N.Y.: Kraus Reprint, 1970.

Groce, George C. *Dictionary of Artists in America, 1564–1860.* New Haven, Conn.: Yale Univ. Pr., 1957.

Grove, Sir George. *Dictionary of Music and Musicians.* New York: St. Martin's, 1975.

Guide to American Directories. 11th ed. Coral Springs, Fla.: Klein, 1982.

Hastings, James, ed. *Encyclopedia of Religion and Ethics.* New York: Scribner, 1908–27.

Historical Abstracts. Santa Barbara, Calif.: ABC-Clio Information Services, 1955– .

Holmes, Frank. *Directory of the Ancestral Heads of New England Families, 1620–1700.* Baltimore: Genealogical Publishing, 1964.

Hotten, John C. *The Original Lists of Persons of Quality, 1600–1700.* Baltimore: Genealogical Publishing, 1983.

International Encyclopedia of the Social Sciences. New York: Crowell, Collier, and Macmillan, 1968.

Journal of American History. New York: Natl. Historical Soc., 1907– .

Kentucky Ancestors. Frankfort: Kentucky Historical Soc., 1965– .

Lasher, George William. *The Ministerial Directory of the Baptist Churches in the United States of America.* Oxford: Ministerial Directory, 1899.

Leaders in Education. 5th ed. New York: Bowker, 1974.

Lossing, Benson John. *The Pictorial Fieldbook of the Revolution.* Rutland, Vt.: Tuttle, 1972.

Madison, Charles Allan. *Eminent American Jews: 1776 to the Present.* New York: Unger, 1970.

Martindale-Hubbell Law Directory. 117th ed. Summit, N.J.: Martindale-Hubbell, 1985.

Mayflower Quarterly. Plymouth, Mass.: General Soc. of Mayflower Descendants, 1935– .

Mennonite Encyclopedia. Hillsboro, Kans.: Mennonite Brethren Publishing, 1955–59.

Methodist Episcopal Church. *Minutes of the Annual Conferences, 1773–1835.* New York: Methodist Episcopal Church, 1840.

Milner, Anita Cheek. *Newspaper Genealogical Column Directory.* Bowie, Md.: Heritage, 1985.

Mississippi Valley Historical Review. Urbana, Ill.: Mississippi Valley Historical Assn., 1914–64.

National Cyclopedia of American Biography. New York: White, 1892– .

National Genealogical Society Quarterly. Washington, D.C.: Natl. Genealogical Soc., 1912– .

New England Historical and Genealogical Register. Boston: New England Historic Genealogical Soc., 1847– .

New York Genealogical and Biographical Record. New York: Genealogical and Biographical Record, 1896.

New York Times Biographical Edition: A Compilation of Current Biographical Information of General Interest. New York: Arno, 1971– .

New York Times Obituaries Index, 1858–1968. New York: New York Times, 1970.

Newspaper Index: The Chicago Tribune, the Los Angeles Times, the New Orleans Times Picayune, the Washington Post. Wooster, Ohio: Newspaper Indexing Ctr., Bell and Howell, 1972– .

Notable American Women: A Biographical Dictionary. Cambridge, Mass.: Belknap, 1971.

Notable American Women, The Modern Period: A Biographical Dictionary. Cambridge, Mass.: Belknap, 1980.

Peterson, Clarence Stewart. *Consolidated Bibliography of County Histories in Fifty States in 1961.* Baltimore: Genealogical Publishing, 1973.

Poole's Index to Periodical Literature, 1802–1906. Boston: Osgood, 1882–1908.

Shepherd, William. *Historical Atlas.* 9th ed. New York: Barnes and Noble, 1964.

South Carolina Historical Magazine. Charleston: South Carolina Historical Soc., 1900– .

Spear, Dorothea N. *Bibliography of American Directories through 1860.* Worcester, Mass.: American Antiquarian Society, 1961; Westport, Conn.: Greenwood, 1978.

Sperry, Kip. *Index to Genealogical Periodical Literature, 1960–77.* Detroit: Gale, 1979.

——. *A Survey of American Genealogical Periodicals and Periodical Indexes.* Detroit: Gale, 1978.

Sprague, William Buell. *Annals of the American Pulpit; or Commemorative Notices of Distinguished Clergymen of Various Denominations from the Early Settlement of the Country to the Close of the Year 1855.* New York: Carter, 1957–69; New York: Arno, 1969.

Taylor's Encyclopedia of Government Officials: Federal and State. Westfield, N.J.: Political Research, 1967– .

Virginia Genealogist. Washington, D.C.: Dorman, 1957– .

Virkus, Frederick Adams, ed. *The Abridged Compendium of American Genealogy.* Chicago: Marquis, 1925; Baltimore: Genealogical Publishing, 1987.

Watkins, Mildred de W. S. *Ancestor Hunting.* Baton Rouge, La.: Claiton's, 1969.

Webster's Biographical Dictionary. Springfield, Mass.: Merriam, 1980.

Who Was Who During the American Revolution. Indianapolis: Bobbs-Merrill, 1976.

Who's Who in American Politics. New York: Bowker, 1967– .

Who's Who in Library and Information Services. Ed. by Joel M. Lee. Chicago: ALA, 1982.

Willard, Frances Elizabeth. *Women of the Century.* Detroit: Gale, 1967.

William and Mary Quarterly. Williamsburg, Va.: Institute of Early American History and Culture, 1892– .

Witney, Henry F. *Biographical Dictionary of American Architects Deceased.* Westport, Conn.: Greenwood, 1976.

Wynder, Bohdan S., ed. *ARBA Guide to Biographical Dictionaries.* Littleton, Colo.: Libraries Unlimited, 1986.

——. *ARBA Guide to Subject Encyclopedias and Dictionaries.* Littleton, Colo.: Libraries Unlimited, 1986.

Chapter 5

Concluding the Search

The ancestors of most Americans came from overseas. Depending on many factors—the relatively recent date of immigration, success in tracing lineage far back, energy and perseverance—sooner or later the researcher will be faced with the decision to continue the search beyond these shores.

Genealogists agree that one should not attempt an overseas search until she or he has made sure that all sources available in this country have been exhausted and that the exact locale of the original family home has been pinpointed. It may also be necessary to consult with the embassy or consulate of the country to be visited. One should check with family members and friends in this country who may know someone in the country of origin who has kept good family records.

Pine suggests in his article on the subject of genealogy in the 1984 edition of *Collier's Encyclopedia* that, because of the many complications of foreign genealogy, search overseas is best left in the hands of a professional genealogist. A knowledge of history, geography, and law is important when searching overseas, and a facility with a foreign language is a must. Available records vary from country to country, depending, to a great degree, on the history of the country. Generally, however, records before the 1400s were not organized, and during earlier times, people had only one name, which compounds the problem of searching old records.

Reconciling dates when going from one calendar system to another is a problem encountered in advanced genealogical research. In 1582, the Julian calendar, introduced by Julius Caesar and based on calculations of the moon's phases, was replaced by the Gregorian calendar in all of the Roman Catholic countries. Until the new calendar was universally used, birth dates may have been misstated by a year.

46

For example, when the new-style calendar was adopted by Great Britain and the colonies in 1752, George Washington, America's first president, along with most persons living under British rule, added eleven days (ten days for those born before February 29, 1700) to his old birth date, resulting in the February 22, 1732, birth date recorded in the history books.[1] Several countries did not adopt the new calendar until the 20th century; Greece adopted it as late as 1923.

GENERAL FOREIGN RESEARCH

Research in foreign countries should begin in American libraries and records depositories. Many documents that can help with overseas searching are housed in the National Archives and in the Library of Congress. The Latter-day Saints Library in Salt Lake City contains the most foreign information because of an extensive microfilming project. This library also houses genealogical periodicals from all over the world.

General Guides

Beard's *How to Find Your Family Roots* contains a large section on tracing family history abroad. It names archives, libraries, record offices, genealogical societies, and helpful books and articles on Africa, Central America, North America, South America, Asia, Australia, New Zealand, the Caribbean, Europe, and the islands of the Pacific. Maralyn Wellauer's *A Guide to Foreign Genealogical Research* gives bibliographies of books on surnames, passenger lists, as well as addresses for genealogical societies, libraries, and archives around the world. Other general guides to overseas research are Westin's *Finding Your Roots: How Every American Can Trace His Ancestors at Home and Abroad*, Neagles' *Locating Your Immigrant Ancestor*, and Pine's *American Origins*. Pine's *Genealogists' Encyclopedia* contains mostly British but also some Latin American and Oriental sources.

Specific Guides

De Platt's *Genealogical Historical Guide to Latin America* covers the 20 countries of Central and South America and the Caribbean countries that once were under Spanish or Portuguese rule. Some coun-

---

1. George O. Zabriskie, *Climbing Your Family Tree Systematically* (Salt Lake City: Parliament Pr., 1969), p.147.

tries are treated in greater detail than others. Obal's *A Bibliography for Genealogical Research Involving Polish Ancestry* includes lists of books and articles, research methodology, and many other aspects of Polish genealogical research. Miller's *Genealogical Research for Czech and Slovak Americans* does the same thing as Obal's work but for Czechs and Slovaks. Similarly, Terrence Punch provides information on genealogical research into immigrants to Nova Scotia in his *Genealogical Research in Nova Scotia*; Charles Hall does so for Germans in *The Atlantic Bridge to Germany*; and David Gardner does the same for the British and Welsh in *Genealogical Research in England and Wales*.

International Libraries

The research process in foreign libraries is similar to that undertaken in American libraries. The locations of libraries in different countries may be obtained from the *International Library Directory: A World Directory of Libraries*.

The national libraries of the countries of interest should be visited since they hold the widest range of materials. For specific primary records, the library and record offices of the ancestral town will yield the best results.

Immigration Records

The pursuit of foreign genealogy involves the same step-by-step approach as that of American genealogy, beginning with primary records and working through secondary sources. The first step is to locate the family in the ancestral country.

Searching family papers in America or passenger arrival lists found either at home or abroad should pinpoint the ancestral home. Books on immigration range from the general, such as Neagles' *Locating Your Immigrant Ancestor*, Miller's *Migration, Emigration, Immigration*, and Tepper's *Passengers to America*, to the very specific, as in *Port Arrivals and Immigrants to the City of Boston 1715 and 1716 and 1762–9*, the U.S. State Department's *Passenger Lists of Vessels Arriving at New York, 1820–97*, Ghirelli's *A List of Emigrants from England to America, 1682–1692*, and others.

Many customs and immigration lists are available, but many gaps exist in the lists. In order to use them, one must already know such information as family name, port, vessel, and date of arrival. Lancour's guide to published lists of early immigrants to North America contained in his *A Bibliography of Ship Passenger Lists, 1538–1825* may prove helpful. He also lists the passenger arrival records housed in the National Archives. P. William Filby and Mary Meyer have compiled a *Passenger and Immigration Lists Index* and *Supplement* covering the 17th, 18th, and 19th centuries.

Names

Name changes present special problems in any genealogical search. Adoptions and other name changes are addressed in *An Index to Changes of Name. . . 1760–1901* by Phillimore and Fry.

The American Council of Learned Societies has published a book titled *Surnames in the United States Census of 1790* analyzing the national origins of the American population at the time of the 1790 census. Hook's *Family Names: How Our Surnames Came to America* contains background information on immigrants to the United States from many areas of the world.

Helmbold's *Tracing Your Ancestry* contains a bibliographical section on surnames from various countries. Other useful works include Dolan's *English Ancestral Names: The Evolution of the Surname from Medieval Occupations*; Bardsley's *A Dictionary of English and Welsh Surnames, with Special American Instances*; and *The Romance of Spanish Surnames* by Maduell.

Manuscripts

Manuscript collections of handwritten documents dealing with early American history are available in libraries and archives. These documents may have been written by individual citizens or by officials in Britain who were charged with the administration of the colonies. The documents have been gathered and preserved for original research by scholars and historians, and may be located through such sources as *Guide to the Manuscript Materials Relating to American History in the German State Archives* by Learned; Matteson's *List of Manuscripts Concerning American History Preserved in European Libraries*; the *Union List of Manuscripts in Canadian Repositories*; and Griffin's *A Guide to Manuscripts Relating to American History in British Repositories Reproduced for the Division of Manuscripts of the Library of Congress*.

Handwriting

A guide intended to help patrons read manuscripts and to some extent to date and localize them is *Handwriting in England and Wales* by Denholm-Young. The subject of handwriting is also addressed in *A Genealogical and Demographic Handbook of German Handwriting, 17th–19th Centuries* by Norman Storrer.

Newspapers and Periodicals

The United States Library of Congress publication *Newspapers in Microform: Foreign Countries, 1948–1972* lists almost 9,000 titles available in American and foreign libraries. *Benn's Guide to Newspapers and Periodicals of the World*, published in London in 1846, leans heavily toward the British Commonwealth and the British Isles. It also contains bibliographical information about other foreign newspapers.

Listing both English- and French-language periodicals, the *Canadian Periodical Index* is comparable to the *Readers' Guide*. The *British Humanities Index* compares with the *Social Sciences and Humanities Index* published in America. An international index to periodicals is the *Internationale Bibliographie der Fremdsprachigen Zeitschriftenliteratur*.

Directories

The *International Bibliography of Directories* contains references to more than 6,000 directories within 50 subject fields. Ancestors known to be outstanding in a certain subject may be searched through an appropriate directory. Universities of the world are listed in *The World of Learning*. The *Worldwide Chamber of Commerce Directory* is useful for locating chambers of commerce in different countries. Chambers of commerce distribute free literature about places, including their history, their libraries, their public records offices, etc.

Biography

The Library of Congress publication *Biographical Sources for Foreign Countries*, designed to give biographical information about living people, includes such sources as monographs, registers of governments, city directories, yearbooks, and many other sources arranged by class, author, and subject. Reliable biographies of prominent people may be found in the *International Who's Who, McGraw-Hill's Encyclopedia of World Biography*, and *Biographie Universelle (Michaud) Ancienne et Moderne*. Biographies for specific geographical areas are represented by such titles as *Who's Who in Canada, Who's Who in Latin America, Who's Who in Communist China*, and *Dictionary of Scandinavian Biography*.

Subject biographies are exemplified by *Authors and Writers' Who's Who*, which is limited to writers of all types in the English-speaking world, and *European Authors, 1000–1900*. Other specific subject biographies include such diverse titles as *International Directory of Anthropologists*, Ireland's *Index to Scientists of the World from Ancient to Modern Times*, Stevenson's *Nobel Prize Winners in Medicine and Physiology, 1901–1950*, Bradley's *Dictionary of Miniaturists, Illuminators, Calligraphers, and Copyists*, and Champlin and Perkins' *Cyclopedia of Painters and Paintings*.

ENGLISH-AMERICAN RESEARCH

Since many of our ancestors came from British soil, and the language of our country is the same, it is easier to search for British ancestors than for ancestors from other countries. In her article "Practical Aspects of Conducting Research in British Libraries and Archives," Michele L. Fagan covers such details as policies for photocopying and obtaining letters of recommendation for researchers. Her bibliography contains many useful references to libraries and archives.

Libraries

The British Museum (now British Museum/Library) is comparable to our Library of Congress, but it is much older and larger. The British Museum's Catalog, which lists holdings of the British Museum, is very similar to the Library of Congress' *National Union Catalog*. Fortescue's *Subject Index of the Modern Works Added to the Library of the British Museum in the Years 1881–1900* lists pages of titles on genealogy and heraldry in many different countries. Peddie's *Subject Index of Books* is also useful for determining types of holdings. Details of local collections in British libraries can be found in the *Libraries, Museums and Art Galleries Yearbook*.

Harvey's *Genealogy for Librarians* is a guide to the resources available for searching in England. Other useful guides to sources are Kaminkow's *A New Bibliography of British Genealogy* and Hamilton-Edwards' *Tracing Your British Ancestors; A Guide to Genealogical Sources*. Harrison's *A Select Bibliography of English Genealogy with Brief Lists for Wales, Scotland, and Ireland* is a source manual followed by a list by counties. Colwell's *Tracing Your Family Tree* is a general "how to" book on British genealogy. These sources are available in both American and British libraries.

Collective Family Histories

The *National Genealogical Directory*, available in libraries, is a guide to the histories of many English families. Other titles of interest are Thomson's *A Catalog of British Family Histories*, Whitmore's *A Genealogical Guide; An Index to British Pedigrees*, and Barrow's *The Genealogists' Guide: An Index to Printed British Pedigrees and Family Histories, 1950–1975*.

Public Record Office

The Public Record Office, located in London, is the British national records repository, or archives. It contains millions of documents from the 11th century to the present. Many of the documents housed in the Public Record Office pertain to American history, especially to the American Revolution.

Most of the records held in the Public Record Office can be used for the study of family history. These records—the most commonly used being chancery proceedings, tax returns, and death registers and indexes—are described by Cox and Padfield in their *Tracing Your Ancestors in the Public Record Office*. Brief descriptions of classes of records found in the Public Record Office can be found in the publications *Guide to the Contents of the Public Record Office; Records of the Colonial and Dominions Offices; Guide to the Material for American History to 1783, In the Public Record Office of Great Britain*; and *Guide to Manuscripts Relating to America in Great Britain and Ireland*.

Guides to Primary Records

Burke's *Key to the Ancient Parish Registers of England and Wales* is a guide to the accessibility of records before 1813. Records before 1837 are located in registers of clergymen or in district record offices. Addresses of these offices can be found in the publications *Record Repositories of Great Britain: A Topographical Directory* and *Record Offices: How to Find Them*. Indexes of births, marriages, and deaths since 1837 in England may be examined in St. Catherine's House and Alexandra House in London. The Genealogical Society of Utah has compiled on microfiche an index of many British baptisms and marriages.

British census records from 1841 to 1881 are available on microfilm in the Census Room, Land Registry Building, London, and other locations as indicated by Gibson's *Census Returns on Microfilm*.

Censuses of 1891 and 1901 are available in the General Register Office in London.

Copies of registered wills dating from 1858 may be examined at the Principal Registry of the Family Division, Somerset House, London. Wills dated before 1858 may be inspected at the Borthwick Institute of Historical Research in York or in other locations, as A. J. Camp outlines in his book *Wills and Their Whereabouts*. Another useful book on British wills is Gibson's *Wills and Where to Find Them*. Kaminkow's book *Genealogical Manuscripts in British Libraries* is indexed by family names, places, authors, and subjects.

Guides to Secondary Sources

Willing's Press Guide, an annual publication distributed in the United States by Bowker, concentrates on British newspapers. *The Times* of London, published from 1906 to the present, serves as England's national newspaper. It is well indexed by the *Official Index to the Times*.

Guides to newspapers include *Census of British Newspapers and Periodicals, 1620–1800; Tercentenary Handlist of English and Welsh Newspapers, Magazines, and Reviews, 1620–1920*; and *Freshest Advices: Early Provincial Newspapers in England*.

Current British Directories contains a subject index to about 2,000 directories that emphasize regional, telephone, county, and subject specialty directories. Universities and colleges are covered by *The Commonwealth Universities Yearbook*, published in London.

Biographies of prominent British citizens can be found in the traditional biographies noted elsewhere. An unusual depth to the subject of British biography is provided by Jerome Reel in his *Index to Biographies of Englishmen, 1000–1485, Found in Dissertations and Theses*.

Professional Service

Guidance is provided to genealogists by the staff at the Public Record Office. Additional help can be obtained through membership in the Society of Genealogists, located in London, which maintains a library and publishes the *Genealogists' Magazine*. The Federation of Family History Societies can provide information on local genealogical societies; it also publishes pamphlets. The Association of Genealogists and Record Agents can provide information about qualified genealogists.

HEREDITARY ORGANIZATIONS; HERALDRY

During the 11th century, a system of heraldry developed in each European country, and some American families are entitled to coats of arms, as William Crozier points out in his book *A Registry of American Families Entitled to Coat Armor*. The chapter on heraldry in the American Genealogical Research Institute's *How to Trace Your Family Tree* tells how to legitimately acquire coats of arms. The College of Arms in London and the Cronistas de Armas in Madrid will make grants of new arms to individuals who apply and who are willing to pay the fees.

Many individuals who work on their own genealogies hope to culminate their work by qualifying for membership in a hereditary society or for a coat of arms. Qualification for membership in a society does not ensure acceptance, as membership in some of the groups is limited in number. Names, addresses, and membership requirements for hereditary societies can be found in the *Hereditary Register*, published since 1972 by Hereditary Publications. Historical background on various hereditary societies may be obtained through Davies' *Patriotism on Parade: The Story of Veterans' and Hereditary Organizations in America, 1783–1900* and by Hood's *American Orders and Societies and Their Decorations*.

The name "Burke" is synonymous with the study of heraldry. Most libraries hold some of the Burke publications. Perhaps the most popular is *Burke's Genealogical and Heraldic History of the Peerage, Baronetage, and Knightage*. Many other books on the subject may be consulted, such as Briggs' *National Heraldry of the World*, Franklyn and Tanner's *Encyclopedic Dictionary of Heraldry*, and Summers' *How to Read a Coat of Arms*. Some peerages have become extinct, as noted in Burke's *Genealogical History of the Dormant, Abeyant, Forfeited, and Extinct Peerages of the British Empire* and Pine's *The New Extinct Peerage 1884–1971, Containing Extinct Abeyant, Dormant and Suspended Peerages, with Genealogies and Arms*.

PUBLICATION

The actual documenting of the material gathered can be the most difficult job of all, but help is available as suggested in Chapter 2. Skills specific to the genealogy writer are covered in the basic "how to" books. Janice Dixon and Dora Flack suggest in *Preserving Your Past*, after the sections on writing and polishing the draft, ways of

CONCLUDING THE SEARCH   55

reproducing the story. Meredith Colke's advice on publishing the genealogy appears in the article "Creating a Worthwhile Family Genealogy," in the December 1968 issue of the *National Genealogical Society Quarterly*. Barnett's *How to Publish Genealogical and Historical Records* is written for the genealogist who's interested in privately publishing his or her family history.

Most genealogies are privately published or reproduced. They may be typewritten and photocopied, mimeographed, or reproduced on a word processor. The Genealogical Publishing Company sells a "do-it-yourself" book titled *My Family Heritage* that is filled in by the researcher. The author may also pay to have his or her work reproduced by a private printing company or by a private publisher.

A family history that has been well compiled and written might be included by a publisher in a collection, or the history of a famous family might be published separately. If a professional job of publishing is desired, the genealogist should contact publishers who specialize in genealogy, such as those listed in the Appendix of this book.

SELECTED BIBLIOGRAPHY

American Council of Learned Societies. *Surnames in the United States Census of 1790; An Analysis of National Origins of the Population.* Baltimore: Genealogical Publishing, 1969.

American Genealogical Research Institute. *How to Trace Your Family Tree.* New York: Doubleday, 1975.

American Society of Genealogists. *Genealogical Research: Method and Sources.* Washington, D.C.: The Society, 1983.

Authors and Writers' Who's Who. 6th ed. Ed. by L. G. Pine. Darien, Conn.: Hafner, 1971.

Bardsley, W. W. *A Dictionary of English and Welsh Surnames, with Special American Instances.* Baltimore: Genealogical Publishing, 1980.

Barnett, Mitzi. *How to Publish Genealogical and Historical Records.* Fort Worth: American Reference, 1971.

Beard, Timothy Field. *How to Find Your Family Roots.* New York: McGraw-Hill, 1977.

Benn's Guide to Newspapers and Periodicals of the World. London: Benn Bros., 1846– .

Biographie Universelle (Michaud) Ancienne et Moderne. Paris: Mme. C. Desplaces, 1843–65.

Bradley, John William. *A Dictionary of Miniaturists, Illuminators, Calligraphers, and Copyists.* London: Quaritch, 1887–9; New York: Burt Franklin, 1958.

Briggs, Geoffrey. *National Heraldry of the World.* London: Dent, 1973.

British Humanities Index. London: Library Assn., 1962–   .

British Museum. Department of Printed Books. *General Catalog of Printed Books.* London: W. Clowes, 1965–6.

———. ———. ———. *Ten-Year Supplement, 1956–1965.* London: Trustees of the British Museum, 1968.

———. ———. *Subject Index of the Works Added to the Library of the British Museum in the Years 1881–1900.* London: Trustees of the British Museum, 1881–.

British Museum-Library. *General Catalogue of Printed Books: Compact Edition. Basic Catalogue (to 1955).* New Canaan, Conn.: Readex, 1967.

Burke, Arthur Meredyth. *Key to the Ancient Parish Registers of England and Wales.* London: Sackville Pr., 1908.

Burke, Sir John Bernard. *Genealogical History of the Dormant, Abeyant, Forfeited, and Extinct Peerages of the British Empire.* London: Harrison, 1883.

Burke's Genealogical and Heraldic History of the Peerage, Baronetage and Knightage. London: Burke's Peerage, 1826–   .

Camp, A. J. *Wills and Their Whereabouts.* n.p.: Published by the author, 1974.

Canadian Periodical Index. Ottawa: Canadian Library Assn., 1948–   .

Census of British Newspapers and Periodicals, 1620–1800. New Castle, Del.: Oak Knoll, 1979.

Chambers Biographical Dictionary. Ed. by J. O. Thorne. New York: St. Martin's, 1969.

Champlin, John Denison, and Charles C. Perkins. *Cyclopedia of Painters and Paintings.* New York: Scribner, 1892; New York: Empire State Bks., 1927.

Colke, Meredith B. "Creating a Worthwhile Family Genealogy." *National Genealogical Society Quarterly* 56, no. 4 (December 1968): 243–62.

Colwell, Stella. *Tracing Your Family Tree.* London: Faber and Faber, 1984.

Commonwealth Universities Yearbook. London: Assn. of the British Commonwealth, 1914–   .

Cox, J. M., and T. R. Padfield. *Tracing Your Ancestors in the Public Record Office.* London: Her Majesty's Stationery Office, 1983.

Crozier, William Armstrong. *A Registry of American Families Entitled to Coat Armor.* New York: Genealogical Assn., 1904.

Current British Directories. 6th ed. New York: Internatl. Publns., 1970.

Davies, Wallace Evans. *Patriotism on Parade: The Story of Veterans' and Hereditary Organizations in America, 1783–1900.* Cambridge: Harvard Univ. Pr., 1955.

De Platt, Lyman. *Genealogical Historical Guide to Latin America.* Detroit: Gale, 1978.

Denholm-Young, Noel. *Handwriting in England and Wales.* Cardiff: Univ. of Wales Pr., 1954.

Dictionary of Scandinavian Biography. London: Melrose Pr., 1972.

Dixon, Janice T., and Dora D. Flack. *Preserving Your Past: A Painless Guide to Writing Your Autobiography and Family History.* Garden City, N.Y.: Doubleday, 1977.

Dolan, J. R. *English Ancestral Names: The Evolution of the Surname from Medieval Occupations.* New York: Potter, 1972.

European Authors, 1000–1900. Ed. by Stanley J. Kunitz. New York: Wilson, 1967.

Fagan, Michele L. "Practical Aspects of Conducting Research in British Libraries and Archives." *RQ* 26 (Spring 1987): 370–5.

Filby, P. William, and Mary K. Meyer. *Passenger and Immigration Lists Index.* Detroit: Gale, 1981.

Fortescue, George H., ed. *Subject Index of the Modern Works Added to the Library of the British Museum in the Years 1881–1900.* London: Pordes, 1966.

Franklyn, Julian, and John Tanner. *An Encyclopedic Dictionary of Heraldry.* Oxford: Pergamon, 1970.

Freshest Advices: Early Provincial Newspapers in England. Ohio State Univ. Pr., 1965.

Gardner, David E. *Genealogical Research in England and Wales.* Logan, Utah: Everton, 1956.

Genealogists' Magazine: Official Organ of the Society of Genealogists. London: The Society, 1925– .

Ghirelli, Michael. *A List of Emigrants from England to America, 1682–92.* Baltimore: Magna Carta, 1968.

Gibson, J. S. W. *Census Returns on Microfilm: A Directory to Local Holdings.* Plymouth, England: Federation of Family History Societies, 1983.

———, comp. *Wills and Where to Find Them.* Chichester: Phillimore, 1974.

Griffin, Grace G. *A Guide to Manuscripts Relating to American History in British Repositories Reproduced for the Division of Manuscripts of the Library of Congress.* Washington, D.C.: Library of Congress, 1946.

Guide to Manuscripts Relating to America in Great Britain and Ireland. Westport, Conn.: Meckler, 1979.

Guide to the Contents of the Public Record Office. London: Her Majesty's Stationery Office, 1964.

Guide to the Material for American History to 1783, in the Public Record Office of Great Britain. Millwood, N.Y.: Kraus Reprint, 1912–14.

Hall, Charles M. *The Atlantic Bridge to Germany.* Logan, Utah: Everton, 1974–78.

Hamilton-Edwards, Gerald Kenneth Savery. *Tracing Your British Ancestors; A Guide to Genealogical Sources.* New York: Walker, 1967.

Harrison, Howard Guy. *A Select Bibliography of English Genealogy with Brief Lists for Wales, Scotland, and Ireland.* London: Phillimore, 1937.

Helmbold, F. Wilbur. *Tracing Your Ancestry: A Step-by-Step Guide to Researching Your Family History.* Birmingham, Ala.: Oxmoor, 1976.

Hereditary Register. Washington, D.C.: Hereditary Publns., 1972– .

Hood, Jennings, and Charles T. Young. *American Orders and Societies and Their Decorations.* Philadelphia: Bailey, Banks and Biddle, 1917.

Hook, J. N. *Family Names: How Our Surnames Came to America.* New York: Macmillan, 1982.

International Bibliography of Directories. New York: Bowker, 1972.

58   CONCLUDING THE SEARCH

International Directory of Anthropologists. 3rd ed. Washington, D.C.: American Anthropological Assn., 1950.

International Library Directory: A World Directory of Libraries. London: Wales, 1963.

International Who's Who. London: Europa Publns., 1938– .

Internationale Bibliographie der Fremdsprachigen Zeitschriftenliteratur aus allen Gebieten des Wissens. Osnabrück: Dietrich, 1963–83.

Ireland, Norma Olin. *Index to Scientists of the World from Ancient to Modern Times.* Boston: Faxon, 1962.

Kaminkow, Marion J. *Genealogical Manuscripts in British Libraries, A Descriptive Guide.* Baltimore: Magna Carta, 1967.

——. *A New Bibliography of British Genealogy, with Notes.* Baltimore: Magna Carta, 1965.

Lancour, Harold. *A Bibliography of Ship Passenger Lists, 1538–1825: A Guide to Published Lists of Early Immigrants to North America.* New York: New York Public Library, 1963.

Learned, Marion Dexter. *Guide to the Manuscript Materials Relating to American History in the German State Archives.* New York: Kraus, 1965.

Libraries, Museums, and Art Galleries Yearbook. Cambridge: Clark, 1981.

Linder, Bill. *How to Trace Your Family History.* New York: Everest, 1978.

Long, Harry Alfred. *Personal and Family Names.* London: Hamilton, Adams, 1883.

McGraw-Hill's Encyclopedia of World Biography. New York: McGraw-Hill, 1973.

Maduell, Charles R. *The Romance of Spanish Surnames.* New Orleans: Privately published, 1967.

Matteson, David Maydole. *List of Manuscripts Concerning American History Preserved in European Libraries and Noted in Their Published Catalogues and Similar Printed Lists.* Washington, D.C.: Carnegie Institute, 1925.

Miller, Olga K. *Genealogical Research for Czech and Slovak Americans.* Detroit: Gale, 1978.

——. *Migration, Emigration, Immigration.* Logan, Utah: Everton, 1977.

National Genealogical Directory. Brighton: Sussex Genealogical Centre, 1979–.

Neagles, James C., and Lila L. Neagles. *Locating Your Immigrant Ancestor: A Guide to Naturalization Records.* Logan, Utah: Everton, 1975.

Notes and Queries: Indexes for Readers, Writers, Collectors and Librarians. New York: B. Franklin, 1970.

Obal, Thaddeus J. *A Bibliography for Genealogical Research Involving Polish Ancestry.* Hillsdale, N.J.: Obal, 1978.

Official Index to the Times. London: Bland, 1914–57.

Peddie, Robert Alexander. *Subject Index of Books Published Up To and Including 1880.* London: Pordes, 1962.

Phillimore, W. P. W., and Edward A. Fry. *An Index to Changes of Name...1760–1901.* London: Phillimore and Fry, 1905.

Pine, L. G. *American Origins: Sources for Genealogical Research and Research Abroad.* Baltimore: Genealogical Publishing, 1980.

_____. *The New Extinct Peerage, 1884–1971, Containing Extinct, Abeyant, Dormant and Suspended Peerages, with Genealogies and Arms.* Baltimore: Genealogical Publishing, 1973.

Port Arrivals and Immigrants to the City of Boston 1715 and 1716 and 1762–9. Baltimore: Genealogical Publishing, 1973.

Punch, Terrence M. *Genealogical Research in Nova Scotia.* Halifax: Petheric Pr., 1978.

Record Repositories of Great Britain: A Topographical Directory. London: Her Majesty's Stationery Office, 1982.

Records of the Colonial and Dominions Offices. London: Her Majesty's Stationery Office, 1964.

Reel, Jerome V. *Index to Biographies of Englishmen, 1000–1485, Found in Dissertations and Theses.* Westport, Conn.: Greenwood, 1975.

Rubincam, Milton. *Genealogical Research: Methods and Sources.* Washington, D.C.: Amer. Soc. of Genealogists, 1980.

Stevenson, Lloyd G. *Nobel Prize Winners in Medicine and Physiology, 1901–1950.* New York: Schuman, 1953.

Storrer, Norman J. *A Genealogical and Demographic Handbook of German Handwriting, 17th–19th Centuries.* Pleasant Grove, Utah: Published by the author, 1977.

Summers, Peter. *How to Read a Coat of Arms.* London: Natl. Council for Social Service, 1967.

Tercentenary Handlist of English and Welsh Newspapers, Magazines, and Reviews, 1620–1920. London: The Times, 1920.

The Times. London: The Times, 1906– .

Union List of Manuscripts in Canadian Repositories. Ottawa: Queen's Printer, 1975.

United States. Department of State. *Passenger Lists of Vessels Arriving at New York, 1820–97.* Washington, D.C.: Dept. of State, 1967.

_____. Library of Congress. *Newspapers in Microform: Foreign Countries, 1948–72.* Washington, D.C.: Library of Congress, 1973.

_____. _____. General Reference and Bibliography Division. *Biographical Sources for Foreign Countries.* Washington, D.C.: Library of Congress, 1944–45.

Wellauer, Maralyn A. *A Guide to Foreign Genealogical Research.* Milwaukee: Wellauer, 1976.

Westin, Jeanne Eddy. *Finding Your Roots: How Every American Can Trace His Ancestors at Home and Abroad.* Los Angeles: Tarcher, 1977.

Who Was Who. New York: St. Martin's, 1953–81.

Who's Who. New York: St. Martin's; London: Black, 1849– .

Who's Who in Canada. Toronto: Internatl. Pr., 1922– .

Who's Who in Communist China. Hong Kong: Union Research Institute, 1971.

Who's Who in Latin America. Detroit: Blaine Ethridge Bks., 1971.

Wiles, R. M. *Freshest Advices: Early Provincial Newspapers in England.* Columbus: Ohio State Univ. Pr., 1965.

Willing's Press Guide. London: Willing, 1874– .

World of Learning. 35th ed. New York: Unipub, 1985.

Worldwide Chamber of Commerce Directory. Loveland, Colo.: Johnson Pubs., 1965–   .

Zabriskie, George O. *Climbing Your Family Tree Systematically.* Salt Lake City: Parliament Pr., 1969.

Appendix

Directory of Organizations and Societies

ARCHIVES AND RECORDS CENTERS

Federal Record Center
24000 Avila Road
Laguna Niguel, California 92677
Tel: (714) 643-4220

Federal Record Center
1000 Commodore Drive
San Bruno, California 94066
Tel: (415) 876-9015

Federal Record Center
Building 48, Denver Federal Center
Denver, Colorado 80225
Tel: (303) 236-0804

Federal Record Center
1557 St. Joseph Avenue
East Point, Georgia 30344
Tel: (404) 647-8744

Federal Record Center
7358 South Pulaski Road
Chicago, Illinois 60629
Tel: (312) 353-0164

Federal Record Center
380 Trapelo Road
Waltham, Massachusetts 02154
Tel: (617) 763-7476

Federal Record Center
2312 East Bannister Road
Kansas City, Missouri 64131
Tel: (816) 926-7271

Federal Record Center
Building 22, MOT Bayonne
Bayonne, New Jersey 07002
Tel: (201) 823-7161

Federal Record Center
3150 Springboro Road
Dayton, Ohio 45439
Tel: (513) 225-2878

Federal Record Center
5000 Wissahickon Avenue
Philadelphia, Pennsylvania 19144
Tel: (215) 951-5588

Federal Record Center
4900 Hemphill Street,
P.O. Box 6216
Fort Worth, Texas 76115
Tel: (817) 334-5515

Federal Record Center
6125 San Point Way, N.E.
Seattle, Washington 89115
Tel: (206) 526–6501

National Record Center
Washington, D.C. 20409
Tel: (301) 763-7000

National Archives and Records
 Administration
Eighth Street and Pennsylvania
 Avenue, N.W.
Washington, D.C. 20408
Tel: (202) 523-3220

Public Record Office
Chancery Lane
London WC2A 1LR
England
Tel: 01-405-0741

HEREDITARY ORGANIZATIONS

American Revolution

Daughters of the Cincinnati
122 East 58th Street
New York, New York 10022
Tel: (212) 751-5168

Descendants of the Signers of the
 Declaration of Independence
50 Riverside Drive
New York, New York 10024

General Society, Sons of the
 Revolution
Fraunces Tavern Museum
54 Pearl Street
New York, New York 10004
Tel: (212) 425-1776

Hereditary Order of Descendants
 of the Loyalists and Patriots of
 the American Revolution
5500 Burling Court
Bethesda, Maryland 20034
Tel: (301) 652-0390

National Society, Daughters of the
 American Revolution
1776 D Street, N.W.
Washington, D.C. 20006
Tel: (202) 628-1776

National Society of the Children
 of the American Revolution
1776 D Street, N.W.
Washington, D.C. 20006
Tel: (202) 638-3153

National Society, Sons of the
 American Revolution
1000 South Fourth Street
Louisville, Kentucky 40203
Tel: (502) 589-1776

Society of the Cincinnati
2118 Massachusetts Avenue, N.W.
Washington, D.C. 20008
Tel: (202) 785-2040

Society of the Descendants of
Washington's Army at Valley
Forge
Box 915
Valley Forge, Pennsylvania 19481
Tel: (617) 335-7670

British

Descendants of the Illegitimate Sons
and Daughters of the Kings of
Britain
107 Lake Lane Rock Creek
Jacksonville, North Carolina 28540
Tel: (919) 324-4954

National Society, Daughters of the
Barons of Runnemede
4530 Connecticut Avenue, N.W.
Washington, D.C. 20008
Tel: (202) 244-6525

Civil War

Auxiliary to Sons of Union Veterans of the Civil War
700 Newark Avenue, Apt. 607
Jersey City, New Jersey 07306
Tel: (201) 795-2230

Children of the Confederacy
328 North Boulevard
Richmond, Virginia 23220
Tel: (804) 355-1636

Dames of the Loyal Legion of the
United States
7809 Navajo Street
Philadelphia, Pennsylvania 19118
Tel: (215) 242-1302

Daughters of Union Veterans of the
Civil War
503 South Walnut Street
Springfield, Illinois 62704
Tel: (217) 544-0616

Ladies of the Grand Army of the
Republic
109 Enola Avenue
Kenmore, New York 14217

Military Order of the Loyal Legion
of the United States
War Library and Museum
1805 Pine Street
Philadelphia, Pennsylvania 19103
Tel: (215) 735-8196

Military Order of the Stars and Bars,
Sons of Confederate Veterans
Box 5164, Southern Station
Hattiesburg, Mississippi 39401
Tel: (601) 582-1621

Sons of Union Veterans of the Civil
War
P.O. Box 24
Gettysburg, Pennsylvania 17325
Tel: (717) 334-1924

United Daughters of the Confederacy
238 North Boulevard
Richmond, Virginia 23220
Tel: (804) 355-1636

Colonial

Colonial Dames of America
421 East 61st Street
New York, New York 10021
Tel: (212) 838-5489

General Society of Colonial Wars
840 Woodbine Avenue
Glendale, Ohio 45246
Tel: (513) 771-8253

General Society of Mayflower Descendants
4 Winslow Street
Plymouth, Massachusetts 02360
Tel: (617) 746-3188

Holland Society of New York
122 East 58th Street
New York, New York 10022
Tel: (212) 758-1675

Jamestowne Society
P.O. Box 7389
Richmond, Virginia 23221

National Society, Colonial Daughters of the 17th Century
10909 Maple Grove
Oklahoma City, Oklahoma 73120
Tel: (405) 751-2134

National Society, Daughters of Founders and Patriots of America
1307 New Hampshire Avenue, N.W.
Washington, D.C. 20036
Tel: (515) 225-6094

National Society, Daughters of the American Colonists
2205 Massachusetts Avenue, N.W.
Washington, D.C. 20008
Tel: (202) 667-3076

National Society of Colonial Dames of America
Dumbarton House 2715 Q Street, N.W.
Washington, D.C. 20007
Tel: (202) 337-2288

National Society, Women Descendants of the Ancient and Honorable Artillery Company
9027 South Damen Avenue
Chicago, Illinois 60620
Tel: (312) 238-0423

Order of the Crown in America
444 Ridgewood Place
Fort Thomas, Kentucky 41075

Order of the Founders and Patriots of America
1701 Massachusetts Avenue, N.W.
Washington, D.C. 20036
Tel: (804) 320-7244

Society of the Descendants of the Colonial Clergy
255 Madison Street
Dedham, Massachusetts 02026
Tel: (617) 326-7457

War of 1812

General Society of the War of 1812
1307 New Hampshire Avenue, N.W.
Washington, D.C. 20036
Tel: (202) 785-2068

National Society, United States Daughters of 1812
1461 Rhode Island Avenue, N.W.
Washington, D.C. 20005
Tel: (202) 332-3181

HISTORICAL AND GENEALOGICAL SOCIETIES

American Association for State and
Local History
708 Berry Road
Nashville, Tennessee 37204
Tel: (615) 383-5991

American Historical Association
400 A Street, S.E.
Washington, D.C. 20003
Tel: (202) 544-2422

American Society of Genealogists
90 East Walnut Street
Belchertown, Massachusetts 01007
Tel: (413) 323-4772

Association of Professional Genealogists
P.O. Box 11601
Salt Lake City, Utah 84147
Tel: (801) 532-3327

Board of Certification of Genealogists
Box 19165
Washington, D.C. 20036

Federation of Family History
Societies
96 Beaumont Street, Milehouse
Plymouth PL2 3AQ
England

Genealogical Society of Utah
50 East North Temple
Salt Lake City, Utah 84150
Tel: (801) 531-4750

National Genealogical Society
1921 Sunderland Place, N.W.
Washington, D.C. 20036
Tel: (202) 785-2123

Oral History Association
P.O. Box 13734, NTSU Station
Denton, Texas 76203
Tel: (817) 565-2026

Organization of American Historians
112 North Bryan Street
Bloomington, Indiana 47401
Tel: (812) 337-7311

Society of Genealogists
37 Harrington Gardens
London SW7 4JX
England
Tel: 01-373-7054

LIBRARIES

American Genealogical
Lending Library
P.O. Box 244
Bountiful, Utah 84019
Tel: (801) 298-5358

British Library
Great Russell Street
London WC1B 3DG
England
Tel: 44-937-8434

Church of Jesus Christ of
Latter-day Saints
Genealogical Library
50 East North Temple Street
Salt Lake City, Utah 84150
Tel: (801) 531-2331

Library of Congress
Local History and Genealogy Reading Room Section
Thomas Jefferson Building, Room LJ244
Washington, D.C. 20540
Tel: (202) 287-5537

Los Angeles Public Library
630 West Fifth Street
Los Angeles, California 90017
Tel: (213) 612-3200

National Genealogical Society Library
1921 Sunderland Place, N.W.
Washington, D.C. 20036
Tel: (202) 785-2123

National Society, Daughters of the American Revolution Library
1776 D Street, N.W.
Washington, D.C. 20006
Tel: (202) 628-1776

New York City Public Library
Fifth Avenue and 42nd Street
New York, New York 10018
Tel: (212) 930-0800

Newberry Library
60 West Walton Street
Chicago, Illinois 60610
Tel: (312) 943-9090

MISCELLANEOUS

Adoptees' Liberty Movement Association
P.O. Box 154
Washington Bridge Station
New York, New York 10033
Tel: (212) 581-1568

Census Microfilm Rental Program
P.O. Box 2940
Hyattsville, Maryland 20784

Military Service Records
National Archives and Records Service
Washington, D.C. 20408
Tel: (202) 523-3220

Publication Sales Branch
National Archives
Washington, D.C. 20408
Tel: (202) 523-3220

PUBLISHERS

Ancestry, Inc.
350 South 400 East, Suite 110
Salt Lake City, Utah 84111
Tel: (801) 687-5628

F. Alton Everest
6275 South Roundhill Drive
Whittier, California 90601
Tel: (213) 698-8831

Everton Publishers, Inc.
Box 368
Logan, Utah 84321
Tel: (801) 752-6022

Gale Research Company
Book Tower
Detroit, Michigan 48226
Tel: (313) 961-2242
Toll Free: (800) 223-4253

Genealogical Books in Print
6818 Lois Drive
Springfield, Virginia 22150
Tel: (703) 971-5877

Genealogical Institute
Dist. by: Family History World
P.O. Box 22045
Salt Lake City, Utah 84122
Tel: (801) 532-3327

Genealogical Publishing Company,
  Inc.
1001 North Calvert Street
Baltimore, Maryland 21202
Tel: (301) 837-8271

Genealogical Sources, Unlimited
7914 Gleason, C-1136
Knoxville, Tennessee 37919
Tel: (615) 690-7831

Kraus Reprint and Periodicals
Route 100
Millwood, New York 10546
Tel: (914) 762-2200

Magna Carta Book Company
5502 Magnolia Avenue
Baltimore, Maryland 21215
Tel: (301) 466-8191

Charles E. Tuttle Company, Inc.
P.O. Box 410
28 South Main Street
Rutland, Vermont 05701
Tel: (802) 773-8229

University Microfilm, Inc.
300 North Zeeb Road
Ann Arbor, Michigan 48106
Tel: (800) 521-0600

Index